# praise for
# they call me pastor

The authors of *They Call Me Pastor* encourage pastors to rejoice
in their calling and to remember always the high privilege of loving
the people God has placed in their care.

**Howard G. Hendricks**
Chairman, Center for Christian Leadership
Distinguished Professor, Dallas Theological Seminary
Dallas, Texas

Every awakening in the Church begins within the hearts and lifestyles of
those who serve and lead the flock. Here is a call to each of us to love, serve,
care for, weep with and rejoice over all Jesus' dear sheep assigned to us.

**Jack W. Hayford**
Founding Pastor, The Church On The Way
President, The King's Seminary
Van Nuys, California

Dr. H. B. London and Dr. Neil Wiseman have written a practical, pertinent and
easy-to-read volume. This is not a stale work by an armchair theoretician, but a
book that breathes with the certain sound of experience and biblical truth.

**Dr. Adrian Rogers**
Pastor, Bellevue Baptist Church
Cordova, Tennessee

There is a small company of gracious and strong men in the kingdom of God
who are pastors of pastors. Here and there the Lord finds men with hearts
after His own heart—men to whom He can entrust the souls of others' pastors and their ministries. I'm grateful two such men have authored this wise
and inspiring volume to help leaders live as fervent followers of Christ, sensitive husbands, devoted fathers and caring shepherds of the flocks of God.

**Ron Mehl**
Pastor, Beaverton Foursquare Church
Beaverton, Oregon

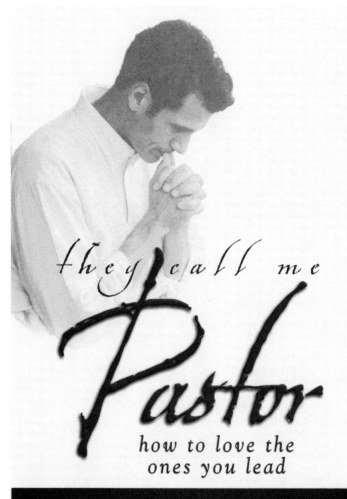

*they call me*

# Pastor

## how to love the
## ones you lead

H.B.
LONDON *&* WISEMAN

NEIL B.

**Regal**
A Division of Gospel Light
Ventura, California, U.S.A.

Published by Regal Books
A Division of Gospel Light
Ventura, California, U.S.A.
Printed in U.S.A.

Regal Books is a ministry of Gospel Light, an evangelical Christian publisher dedicated to serving the local church. We believe God's vision for Gospel Light is to provide church leaders with biblical, user-friendly materials that will help them evangelize, disciple and minister to children, youth and families.

It is our prayer that this Regal book will help you discover biblical truth for your own life and help you meet the needs of others. May God richly bless you.

*For a free catalog of resources from Regal Books/Gospel Light, please call your Christian supplier or contact us at* 1-800-4-GOSPEL *or* www.regalbooks.com.

Cover Design by Barbara LeVan Fisher
Interior Design by Rosanne Richardson
Edited by Becky Jones

Library of Congress Cataloging-in-Publication Data
London, H. B.
    They call me pastor / H.B. London, Jr. and Neil B. Wiseman.
        p. cm.
    Includes bibliographical references.
    ISBN 0-8307-2390-0
    1. Clergy—Office. I. Wiseman, Neil B. II. Title.

BV660.2 .L665 2000
253—dc21                                             00-032339

1  2  3  4  5  6  7  8  9  10  11  12  13  14  15  /  07  06  05  04  03  02  01  00

Rights for publishing this book in other languages are contracted by Gospel Literature International (GLINT). GLINT also provides technical help for the adaptation, translation and publishing of Bible study resources and books in scores of languages worldwide. For further information, contact GLINT, P.O. Box 4060, Ontario, CA 91761-1003, U.S.A. You may also send e-mail to Glintint@aol.com, or visit their website at www.glint.org.

# Contents

## Section 3
## The Leader Who Trusts Through Triumph and Tragedy

## Section 4
## The Minister Who Loves at Home

## Section 5
## In Partnership with the Father

**Section 6**
**The Never-Say-Die Pastor Who Impacts**
**the Third Millennium**

**Epilogue**
**For the Sake of New Beginnings**    

# love your People to greatness

INTRODUCTION

# love your people to greatness

I cannot remember exactly when it was, but it had to be more than 25 years ago that I stood before my congregation and said, "God loves you as though you were the only person in all the world to love. Had he not sent His only Son to die for the whole of the human race, He would have sent Him to die just for you—that makes you a very important person. And I love you too."

Probably that one phrase can be quoted by more members of the congregations I have served than any other. I would often take a moment before the prayer time in a morning worship service and tell them how honored I felt to be their pastor. I thanked them for their patience with me. I valued their comments, learned from their constructive criticism and swelled a bit too much because of their affirmation. Through the more than three decades that I was called pastor, I attempted to have a love affair with my people. I tried never to allow the business of the church to become an us-against-them situation. I had always believed that it was their church. They had prayed for it, sacrificed to see it born and held steady in times of uncertain transition. Who was I to come in and create insecurities for them?

That is not to say I didn't challenge their mind-set. In fact, I was always looking for ways to move them forward, to strengthen their faith and to help them see that taking risks was the only way to make progress. But I did it in love—not so unlike parents who insist their children practice the piano or do their homework or complete their chores around the house. I was con-

LOVE YOUR PEOPLE TO GREATNESS   11

stantly asking them to move up a little—to live outside of their comfort zone. And most of the time they did. The love between us made the difference.

The first time someone called me pastor, it seemed strange. I not only felt too young to carry that title, but I also didn't feel worthy or ready for the responsibilities that accompanied that God-ordained office (see Eph. 4:11). But I grew to love the title and to this day respond to it with joy. It made me feel special when they called me pastor.

Pastor,

> . . . thanks for the sermon.
>
> . . . I need to talk with you.
>
> . . . my mom just died.
>
> . . . we are going to have a baby.
>
> . . . God seems to be directing us to another church.
>
> . . . I believe God has called me into the ministry. How can *I know for sure?*
>
> . . . the X-rays do not look good. Could you pray with me?
>
> . . . we will be moving to the East Coast next week. We will miss you.
>
> . . . when do you think you will have time to get a haircut?
>
> . . . I'm gay . . . what should I do?
>
> . . . we are praying for you.
>
> . . . my wife just left me.
>
> . . . our daughter is pregnant.
>
> . . . thanks for being there when I needed you.

The list is endless, but you know what I mean and how it feels. Whenever the phone rings or there is a knock at your office door or you read a letter, you are ushered into a unique collection of men and women. Unless you have been a pastor, you cannot really understand how ministry can be beautiful and painful at the same time. When it is good, it is wonderful; when it is bad, it can be terrible. But it is the call and the sense of God's unmistakable presence that keeps us from running away.

I have written and spoken often of the following story: I remember having a collision one time with an automobile. I was on a bike-riding excursion with my boys. The incident took place next door to our home. The driver of the car was my neighbor. As I was seated on the pavement—bleeding, angry and surrounded by my two sons, Brad and Bryan, who were terribly embarrassed—the man loomed over me. He was speechless and evidently not thinking straight because he bent down and asked me, "Are you okay?" Of course I wasn't okay. As I was preparing to make my case, his wife came running out of their house screaming at the top of her voice, "Pastor, Pastor, Pastor!" She took one quick look at me and then turned to her husband. She paused a moment, stuck a bony finger up under his nose and in a frantic voice she cried, "See there! See there! You couldn't hit a kid; you had to hit a pastor!" I smile at that now because even in a moment of near disaster, I was singled out as someone special and unique. But I wouldn't change it for the world.

Every calling, including the ministry, has some compelling force and defining relationship. Health brings physician and patients together. Justice brings lawyer and clients together. Learning brings teacher and students together. Love is the life-giving force that brings pastor and parishioners together.

Because our Lord established the Church as His society of love on earth, we pastors have the wonderful privilege to give love, to be loved and to lead others to express Christ's love in the world.

Love's main energizing motive is explained in these strong words from the apostle John: "First we were loved, now we love. He loved us first. . . . The command we have from Christ is blunt:

Loving God includes loving people. You've got to love both"
(1 John 4:19-21, *THE MESSAGE*).

My grandfather, A. S. London, was a very loving shepherd,
and when he wrote about love, he was describing the centerpiece
of his own life. Hear his heart:

> We need the kind of love that meets suspicion with kind-
> ness, and hate with compassionate concern. Love will seek
> out the careless, the unconcerned, and the shiftless. Love
> shows tenderness toward the soiled, the foulest, the pen-
> niless. Love seeks the lost sheep. It goes after the lost coin
> and longs and prays for the prodigal son. The life that
> loves will have its night of sorrow. A man who loves deeply
> will have his midnight hours as well as his season of sun-
> light.[1]

And when he talked of the love of Christ, he reflected:

> It was love that halted the passing funeral and gave a
> young man back his mother. Love stood before the cold
> tomb and spoke words till the sleeping dead hurried from
> the grave to walk among the living. Love crossed a lake to
> cure the demon-possessed. Love bears with dirt, ignorance,
> quarrels, and disputes. It calls to the beggar, the outcast,
> the underprivileged, and offers pardon and purity to all.[2]

> Love watches at the door of the prison cell, to speak a kind
> word and offer a helping hand to one who had lost his
> way. It walks beside the women of the vilest sins and paus-
> es to say a kind word to the one who is helpless. It offers
> hope to all.[3]

My "pop" believed that the gospel of a broken heart demands the ministry of bleeding hearts. "The love of Christ constraineth [compels] us" (2 Cor. 5:14, *KJV*) is the prevailing passion of one who loves.

Loving those we serve is the message of this book. You are the Father's love agents in your church and your world, so "it is clear to us, friends, that God not only loves you very much but also has put his hand on you for something special" (1 Thess. 1:4, *THE MESSAGE*). This book is intended to be an affectionate reminder that without love, ministry quickly turns into an empty charade and a miserable existence. We really believe that one's ministry—your ministry—becomes much more enjoyable and more effective as you increase your love for those you serve. Love makes every expression of ministry better, and it makes you more Christlike.

In so many ways, our ministries are summed up in the poignant oft-quoted announcement: "I shall pass through this world but once. Any good thing, therefore, that I can do, or any act of kindness that I can show to any human being, let me do it now. Let me not defer it or neglect it, for I shall not pass this way again."

From my heart,
H. B. London, Jr.

### Notes

1. A. S. London, *Love Is the Key* (Kansas City, MO: Beacon Hill Press, 1956), p. 13.
2. Ibid.
3. Ibid., p. 25.

# the *Shepherd*

who loves

and

leaves a

legacy

Section 1

# i'll love you forever

I sat in front of the pulpit on the carpeted steps of my church in Pasadena, California. In my hands, I held Robert Munsch's book *I'll Love You Forever*. My voice cracked as I read the moving story of the lifelong love a mother gives to her son. After 31 years of pastoral ministry, I was leaving my church family to become a pastor to pastors at Focus on the Family. How I dreaded that good-bye.

That morning, I gave no thought to my dignity. Not a hint of embarrassment crossed my mind as I looked out on the faces of my large family and told them that no one could ever take their place in my heart. I wanted them to know that I would never forget them. They had made an indelible mark on my heart. Love affects me that way.

There are no promotions from the pastorate, even if you go on to another kind of ministry. Nothing compares to the love bond between a pastor and a congregation. Please believe me—there is nothing like it. So, pastor friend, cherish those close relationships and celebrate the love of those in your church. They love you and they need your love. Be careful not to let the "joy suckers" sour your love for the rest.

I have a congregation-sized hole in my heart that never seems to heal. How I miss having a church family. My work at Focus on the Family allows me to preach in some of America's greatest churches—and I enjoy it immensely. But I miss walking up the aisle, up the steps, onto the platform and into my own pulpit. I miss visiting sick members in the hospital. I miss the tear-filled celebration of "my" young couples' weddings. I miss listening to the last words of love for Christ whispered by those dying saints who have stood by me through thick and thin. I miss preaching the gospel to their friends and neighbors at the funeral service. I miss holding those soft, helpless babies in front of their spiritual family and dedicating them to the loving Shepherd. I miss making visits into the homes of my church members and hearing the words of encouragement they whisper in my ear at the end of the service. Though I realize that those days are gone and though I have a deep satisfaction in my present work, nonetheless, my heart yearns to minister to a group of people who love me and whom I love in return.

Radio host Paul Harvey shares a story about an elderly woman obliged to sell the house where she had lived for years. Before the final papers were signed, she insisted that the new owners come to the house for coffee. As they drank and ate cookies together, she told them that if they were to hear a creak on the steps or the curtain ruffle that they shouldn't be upset, because it's just her presence coming back to relive some memories in the house that she loved so much.

The Sunday I said good-bye, I told my congregation that I would be back to visit in my spirit from time to time. Of course I meant that in my inner spirit, I would walk down the aisle or sit to pray with one or the other. I would remember walking through their valleys with them or singing a little song about Jesus with a sick brother or sister. "You'll have a new pastor," I told them, "and he'll take good care of you. But you can also know that I will always remember your loving ways and the close times we shared."

Pastor friend, soak in the love God gives you through your church. Rejoice that you have a congregation to love. Disappointment may be in your heart right now, but I beg you to open your heart to God's Spirit. Love your people whole-heartedly and without reservations. It saddens me when I hear pastors make cutting remarks about their congregation's idio-syncrasies. Carry ministry relationships as if they were precious china—delicate, elegant and costly. Remember, believers some-times put up with a lot in us. Over and over again in my long years of ministry I have seen members of my church treat me with patient forbearance, wholehearted acceptance and unbe-lievable generosity.

As you increase your love for people your pastoral ministry will be more effective and satisfying. The apostle Paul, in Ephesians 5:2 (THE MESSAGE), calls us to love as Jesus did: "Observe how Christ loved us. His love was not cautious but extravagant. He didn't love in order to get something from us but to give everything of himself to us. Love like that." Congregations love their pastor in direct proportion to the love they receive. Think about ways to let your people know how much you love them.

*Tell the Lord.*
Publicly thank God for the love you receive from your congregation. Neil told me about a pastor who has served the same church for 50 years. In a recent congre-gational prayer, the veteran said, "Thank you for bring-ing us together, keeping us together and teaching us how to love each other." That's quite a prayer after 50 years.

*Preach love as a beautiful gift.*
Go back to Scripture and teach your congregation over and over that our love for one another grows naturally out of our love for God. And our love for God grows out

of His love for us. Preach God's love to your people. Show them that love is a gift we receive from God and pass on to those around us. It is a privilege, never an obligation.

*Demonstrate love in administrative meetings.*
Some churches allow a sad antagonism in decision-making groups. Members say there what they would never say in refined company. Refuse to play that game. If unloving words are expressed in such meetings, direct the conversation back to forgiveness, encouragement and acceptance. Christians can discuss issues without breaking Christ's principles of love. Sometimes you might need to stop the meeting for a brief prayer—"Oh Lord, help us love each other as You love us."

*Train yourself to say "I love you in Christ."*
Love needs actions as well as words. It may sometimes be uncomfortable for male pastors to say "I love you." However, with practice you can say it and mean it. Once you begin using those words, watch to see what happens. My guess? Your church will be transformed.

*Love is a boomerang.*
Of course, pastors should not communicate an artificial, sugary relationship with people. Nor should they use love language as a tool to ward off criticism. However, there is strength in realizing that the people who are loved are easier to serve. Elbert Hubbard, a writer from the last century, said, "The love we give away is the only love we keep."[1] And he is right. When people know you love them, they overlook a multitude of faults.

*Love is absolutely essential in churches.*
Loveless churches are uncomfortable places to visit and stifling places in which to worship. A pastor who does not love people puts a limiting lid on God's work. Martin Buber, a philosopher, probably had pastors in mind when he wrote, "He who loves brings God and the world together."[2] Love is the most crucial factor in Kingdom work.

*Show love anonymously.*
I have a friend, an established photographer, who had a beginning optometrist move into his building. The new eye doctor had trouble meeting his rent. My friend shoved an envelope containing five $100 bills under the young doctor's office door after hours. Later he asked the doctor to remove the lenses from the glasses of customers he was to about to photograph, in order to keep down the glare. The doctor agreed, and soon those same people started buying their glasses from the optometrist. Now the eye doctor is well established but still wonders who gave him $500 in his hour of need.

Real love is always Christlike and beautiful.

—H. B. L.

**Notes**
1. Rebecca Davis and Susan Mesner, eds., *The Treasury of Religious and Spiritual Quotations* (Pleasantville, NY: Reader's Digest Association, 1994), p. 307.
2. Ibid., p. 304.

# "pastor"—what a beautiful word

"Pastor"—it is a beautiful word, and what a unique relationship it represents. Next to the word "love" or being called "Dad," I believe it is the most wonderful word in the English language.

Each time someone calls me pastor, I am still awestruck even after all these years. I still feel honored and amazed by the word. When I hear it, I square my shoulders and renew my purpose. I feel humbled and am grateful, for there is no higher privilege than being a pastor.

To be a pastor is more than fulfilling a job or doing well in an occupation; it is a way of life. It is a lofty vocation, a high calling that most people will never experience. Think of it—out of more than 6 billion people on earth, you were called by the God of heaven. He placed His hand on your shoulder and called you to be a minister. Maybe you jumped at the chance. Maybe you came kicking and screaming. But now God is using you to accomplish His purposes.

Pastoral ministry defined my life, seeping into every cranny of my being and thought. Any comparison to other tasks or roles falls far short of the holy privilege I have as a pastor. I represent the Lord of glory—what an awesome opportunity and amazing honor. God named me to be His incarnational representative in the Church and in His world. That means I represent Him wherever I am. I don't deserve it, and I rely every day on His empowerment and wisdom. But I love being a pastor, and I never want to disappoint the One who called me.

Think about your unique privilege as a pastor. God will help you bloom where He has planted you. He has you in your present assignment so that you can be a life changer there. Even if other pastors have struggled to succeed in the church where you find yourself, God wants to enable you to do something lasting for Him in that place. He promises to empower you to be and do more than you can imagine. His promises show us that we are never alone. What a partnership—what a possibility.

That is why we see our town differently from others as we drive through traffic, thinking of ways to reach our community for Christ. That is why we lie awake into the night hours asking God to show us His will for His church.

I love the story credited to Babe Ruth, who was not by any measure a Christian giant. Ruth said, "I knew an old minister, and how I envied him. I'm listed as a famous home-run hitter, yet beside that obscure minister—who was good and wise—I never made it to first base." God wills each pastor to be good and wise.

I vividly remember the evening I was ordained. The ordinands knelt at the altar at the end of an inspiring service. Around us stood other clergy, and the leaders of my denomination. I was a 24-year-old pastor, with limited potential but a never-say-die attitude. As I felt the hands of my colleagues on my shoulders, I could also feel the strong hand of the One who called me. It was His way of saying, "I have set you apart for Kingdom work, and I promise you My never-failing presence. Son, I will never leave you." And He never has. I would imagine you feel much the same way.

Pastor, think how your title helps shape your ministry.

*Persevere.*
God's call sustains you when the going gets tough. The call energizes every day, whether it is one of victory, of

trial or even the day of final accounting before the Master. The title "pastor" encourages us to stick by our post until we experience a spiritual breakthrough. I believe God has something specific for every pastor to accomplish in every place. If my belief is accurate, then something significant must be accomplished in this assignment before you consider a change. Always consult the Caller before you consider moving.

*Partner.*
A pastor works, cries, prays, counsels, studies, preaches and strives for excellence. I must do my best while always knowing my best is never good enough. However, it is a great comfort to know we are partners with Omnipotence. That makes all the difference. Yet there is no job on earth that so shows you your human weakness. Competence and dependence are two irreducible and winning components for ministry in every setting.

*Motivate.*
The title "pastor" motivates ministry. The love of God invigorates me as I serve His Church. To be loved by those we serve energizes ministry. Our love for people, their love for us; God's love for them, His love for us—this intertwining love connection creates a joy in serving. It also provides a powerhouse of motivation for ministry.

*Stand tall.*
Every time someone calls you pastor, breathe a prayer of thanks: "God, I want to tell You how much I appreciate being in such close relationship with You." And you might add, "Lord, I am sorry for the times I sought pity

or asked for release. Enable me to be in ministry for the long haul."

*Be special to God.*
The title "pastor" makes you realize you are special. When God said, "I want you," it probably startled you as much as it did me. But He has something unique in mind for you to do. No one else knows the abiding promises you and God made at that private moment.

Ron Jones is a pastor in Liverpool, England. When he was only 16 years of age, he woke in the night, sensing a special presence of God. He was convinced in a moment of delightful communion with his Lord that God had promised him he would be a pastor. But Ron had a terrible stutter and saw no possibility of serving God in this capacity. He waited many long years for that promise to come true. Gradually, the Lord prepared Ron. He took away his stutter and taught him to love people by giving him two jobs—that of a debt collector and that of a choir director. At the age of 63, after years of caring for his clients and his choir members, Ron was called by his church to be their pastor. He is now 85 and still pastoring.

So don't forget that special moment when God laid His hand on you and set you apart for a great work. He will keep all His promises. Rely on Him as you serve His people.

—H. B. L.

# offer a holy PRESENCE

Four doctors in surgical greens stood before Dave and Jana at the Huntington Memorial Hospital in Pasadena. I stood by helplessly as one doctor spoke. "Your baby has died of Sudden Infant Death Syndrome," he said quietly. "We want to give you a chance to hold your child before we take her." I watched this young couple, their shoulders shook with emotion, as they held their firstborn for the last time.

My mind raced to find something to say to the shocked young couple. I wanted to tell them that everything would be okay, but that wasn't true. Their baby was dead. All my pastoral training and experience seemed to fail me then. "Dave and Jana," I began, with words that were broken and slow, "I don't know why this awful loss has to come to you. But I know God loves you as if you were the only ones in the whole world to love. If you accept His love . . . if you believe He does love you, you'll make it. If you don't, you won't." Those were the only words I had for them. And they seemed awfully empty at the time.

All I could do was to represent the caring Jesus. I choked back my own emotions while they tried valiantly to cling to their newfound faith. But something happened in that hospital room. Neither the couple nor I had words to erase the pain. But a Holy Presence invaded that place. God joined the three of us. Just as in the Old Testament story of the fiery furnace, when God Himself came to comfort Shadrach, Meshach and Abednego, so we felt in the fiery trial of suffering an assurance that God was caring for us.

That couple didn't expect great words from me. It's a good thing, because I didn't have any. But I knew about God's faithfulness. I knew He was the God of the helpless. I knew He had a thousand ways to strengthen them, even when they felt abandoned. I knew He loved Dave and Jana.

Dave worked for Disney, and Jana worked as a seamstress at Universal Studios. Earlier that year they had experienced a radical, life-transforming conversion. In coming to Christ they had abandoned a cultish background and lost family and friends in the process. I wondered if their new faith would hold in the face of such a trauma. I prayed it would.

In all the pain, I remembered what a precious time we had had a few weeks earlier when we dedicated their baby in the worship service. Now this.

I confess that a few times in my ministry, the whys from my heart have almost made me quit. I am sure you have experienced similar anguish. But in our heart of hearts we know that there is no satisfactory human answer to the problem of evil. I used to try to defend God against the whys, but I quit trying. As Job discovered, some answers are not ours to know this side of eternity.

We had the funeral in a beautiful Southern California setting. We felt for them, hurt for them and cried with them. When the service was over our lives returned to normal, but Dave and Jana continue to struggle with the death of their baby. My heart was so heavy for Dave and Jana—new converts, the death of a child, no explanation. But somehow, God enabled them to remember my faltering encouragement to trust God's love completely. That was all they had.

One day, after coming to Focus on the Family, I received a letter with a picture of Dave and Jana holding a beautiful baby. They wrote, "H. B., you probably don't think we heard you when you encouraged us to cling to the love of God when our baby died. But we heard you clearly. So we have believed over and over that God loves us as if we were the only ones to love."

The letter continued with these victorious words: "H. B., we made it. We have learned to live in the love of God. We quote your words to each other often. The Lord is gracious. Notice in the picture we are holding a beautiful new baby—God's special gift to us. We don't understand why we lost our first child. We still hurt when we think about it, but we don't question God anymore. We live one day at a time in nearness to Him, and we are finding the enabling grace of the Lord is enough."

I have thought a lot about their faith and mine since receiving that letter. Some tough situations are mysteries beyond our comprehension. Mysteries greater than our answers. Mysteries that stretch our faith. Mysteries that force us to turn to God because we can't find answers anywhere else.

My strengthening message for every pastor is that we live close to the mysteries—in fact, we have a front seat. We see God at work in ways we don't understand. The Holy One we represent doesn't always reveal the details of His plans to us. But take heart. Though I felt as if I had no answers for Dave and Jana, my simple words of faith were more than enough.

After thinking about some of the disguised purposes of God, I remembered to read again the incredible promise of 1 Corinthians 13:12 (*THE MESSAGE*): "We don't yet see things clearly. We're squinting in a fog, peering through a mist. But it won't be long before the weather clears and the sun shines bright! We'll see it all then, see it all as clearly as God sees us, knowing him directly just as he knows us!"

Let's consider ways to take the awesome presence of God into the details of our ministry to hurting people:

*You don't have answers for everything.*

Make peace with that fact. Stand in awe with your people as you experience the mysteries of God together. Sometimes preachers find it hard to say, "I don't know." But let's admit that some things are beyond our understanding, "I am not sure what God is doing, but I know He is good."

*Use pastoral care to validate preaching.*

Notice I intentionally used the word "validate." Preaching becomes theoretical and abstract until it is authenticated by a firsthand experience of how faith works in living. If you are too busy to authenticate your preaching by taking Christ to the hurting, bleeding, confused, destitute and dying, you are much too busy to preach. "God talk" from the pulpit without pastoral action in Jesus' name is hollow and often distorted. The shepherding connection with people is as necessary a preparation for preaching as are study, prayer and fasting.

*Rejoice in mysteries.*

The Bible gives us many principles by which we can understand how to live. However, though God does not try to confuse us, He and His ways are not always obvious. His actions are sometimes beyond our capacities to understand and are deeper than our experience. Abraham did not understand why God would ask him to sacrifice the son of the promise, for whom he had waited for so many long years. But he obeyed in faith.

*Preaching is not always in church.*

Some preaching moments are given to a pastor in one-on-one situations. My words about God's faithfulness to

Dave and Jana made a greater impact in that hospital room than they would have from the pulpit. Their sad situation made them ready to hear. God used the fact that I was in the room with them at their moment of despair to enable me to communicate faith. Pastoral care gives us a golden opportunity to repreach in real-life situations what we say about God in our public proclamation.

*Find fulfillment in pastoral care.*
Any veteran pastor describing the most fulfilling moments of ministry will not speak for long before telling you about a time when God used human desperation to draw needy people to Himself. When you have the privilege of representing the Holy One to someone in crisis, you form bonds of affection that last a lifetime. You may even be surprised at the portal of heaven, when Jesus thanks you for standing with Him in the hospital room. "When did I stand in a hospital with you?" I might ask Christ, and He will answer, "When you stood there with Dave and Jana, you were ministering to Me."

*See caring ministry as incarnational.*
Jesus identified with hurting people. Wherever He went, those He served knew that He sat where they sat and felt what they felt. I sometimes wonder what might have happened to Dave and Jana had their pastor not been there. Think how lonely it would be to face agony, pain and death without hearing someone say "Look to Jesus— He's the One who loves you with an everlasting love." Our call and the needs of people compel us to replicate the Incarnation. The apostle Paul said, "God appointed him (Christ Jesus) to be head over everything for the

church, which is his body, the fullness of him who fills everything in every way" (Eph. 1:22). Just as Jesus was God in human flesh, He now asks every pastor to flesh out His compassion and mercy.

—H. B. L.

# they won't change unless they trust you

"Change changes everything"—those words can terrorize any pastor.

Pastors sometimes look down on their congregation if they can't handle a little change. However, if we are candid, we must admit change frightens us as much as it frightens them. Maybe more. Change almost always takes us where we have never been. It makes us feel the church is out of control.

To lower your stress about change, let me suggest two remedies that will reduce fear for everyone. The first antistress medication is to show authentic love for everyone in the congregation, even those who resist change. The second antidote is to appreciate a congregation's uniqueness.

When parishioners know their pastor really loves them, they are far more likely to accept change. When a pastor loves the people in Jesus' name, misunderstandings often dissolve before they start. Scripture declares, "Love . . . bears all things" (1 Cor. 13:7, *NASB*). This dependable biblical promise covers times when you do not understand the position taken by others or when they cannot understand yours.

A pastor must help a congregation remember that a unique past shapes every church's outlook, prospects, needs and future. An effective leader understands this principle and encourages church members to cherish the unique identity God has given them as a congregation. To overlook uniqueness creates unnecessary problems, which lead to resistance and antagonism. So beware of the temptation to borrow a program from a successful church and to plop it without adaptation into your church situation. Effective pastors intentionally design ministries that fit a particular setting.

An old country preacher remarked, "Everything that used to be nailed down is coming apart." Change, whether in the Church, the family or the society, is as real as the oxygen we breathe. It is relentless and it is here to stay.

In our society, we all feel the tides of rapid change washing at the shores of our culture. Technology has pushed the Fast Forward button; and global communication makes ethical and moral changes sweep over the globe in the blink of a TV camera's eye. The reality—change is here whether you welcome, resist or ignore it.

Can change be used to give the Church a brighter tomorrow?

Yes and no. No, if change confuses and threatens us. I always feel sorry to hear of pastors who are so bewildered by change that they either drop out of ministry or continue in quiet desperation. I am equally saddened by pastors who so love the adrenaline rush of change that they grab for the newest fad or the most "in" ministry trend.

I laugh now at the changes I once resisted, like recorded accompaniment or praise choruses. They happened in spite of me. Though I always felt a tinge of disappointment if someone resisted the wonderful changes I proposed, I was sometimes blind to the fact that I resisted the changes others suggested.

To clarify the issue, it is helpful to divide change into three categories: what a church *must never* change, what a church *is free to* change and what a church *must* change.

Of course the changeless must never be changed. In times of rapid transition like ours, it is easy to confuse the abiding with the passing. Ways of doing church change. Procedures change.

Musical forms change. At the same time, the gospel is timeless. Christ is the same yesterday, today and forever. A church that fails to proclaim Jesus Christ—His incarnation, death, resurrection, ascension and return—has changed itself into something other than a church.

However, a church firmly built on Jesus Christ can change many things. Often change is merely improving and repackaging ministry. For example, churches should feel free to bring presentations up to date and to consider how they can make the gospel understandable to a society that has no Christian memory. Such changes are desirable.

Preaching the gospel is a requirement of Scripture and must be done effectively in every generation. It is not an option. But Jesus preached from a boat, while Paul preached in the marketplace. Stephen preached on death row, and Paul preached in an upstairs room, late at night. Preaching styles, sermon length and vocabulary choices will vary from culture to culture and from generation to generation. Communication methods change, but the essential content of the message never does.

In considering what may change without diluting the gospel, the Church must not allow the culture to set her agenda—only Scripture does that. Since Scripture expects the Church to be an alien culture in every society, we must shape ministry not according to what pleases people, but according to what God wants.

When I was growing up, Christians tended to determine worldliness based on the appearance. How was a particular person dressed? Was his tie appropriate? Was the little girl's dress too fancy? Now I realize worldliness has much to do with the secular attitudes of the heart that infiltrate the Church and subtly shape its ministry.

I do a lot of traveling from church to church. I notice that change is good when it maintains the unchangeable nature of the gospel and tailors its celebration and proclamation to the identity of a given congregation. In today's Church world, most pastors have the freedom to fit their methods to the specific needs of their church and community.

That means your ministry does not need to look exactly like someone else's. What a relief to know you do not have to be a clone of another pastor. You were created as a unique pastor. And you have been providentially planted in your assignment to do something special for God. If you stay open to His leading, you will discover what He wants done.

Another element that the Bible allows us to change is style. Style has to do with cultural and personal differences in applying the gospel. How is ministry to be done? How should you preach? How should you keep in contact with your people?

I once watched a video of a church service held in North Africa. The believers took off their shoes before entering the place of worship. They chanted when they read the Scriptures. They had decided to use certain elements of their culture in their worship. But these choices were perfectly acceptable according to biblical principles. Some of the things I would list under style might have to do with how formally or how casually people dress, or whether the service is held on folding chairs on a basketball floor or in plush pews in a cathedral-style church.

What do not change, however, are the basic elements of preaching and caring for people. Let's be blunt—some pastors have given up on pastoral care. They argue that pastoral care is a matter of style—a style they don't have. This is like the Christian college student who excused her selfish behavior to her roommate with this interesting statement: "I don't have the gift of mercy." Such reasoning is a serious mistake.

A pastor cannot give up the responsibility of caring for the wanderer, comforting the bruised, healing the sick and assisting the dying. It is not a question of style. However you do it, caring for people is a basic essential of what it means to be a pastor. This caring component of ministry is rooted in Jesus' teaching and practice. Two verses should close the debate. Jesus says, "Whatever you did for one of the least of these brothers of mine, you did for me" (Matt. 25:40); and He commands Peter to "feed my sheep" (John 21:17). If you feel I might be stating the case too strongly, check your New Testament.

A similar logic can be applied to preaching. There are many ways to do it, but it must be done. I do not consider myself a classical orator, an eloquent preacher or an awe-inspiring exegete. But in my preaching style, I try to speak to people where they live. I talk about their families and their hurts, and I use illustrations that fit their world. I know I have achieved my purpose when someone says, "Pastor, you preached as if I were the only one in the congregation today. God put my address and zip code on your sermon. You were talking to me." In preaching, a pastor is free to use a variety of approaches—that's style.

One's preaching style must draw attention to God. I admit to being troubled by some preachers who pace as they speak. Such a style usually distracts worshipers. I don't pretend to have all the answers, and I don't want to be unloving or dogmatic. But I know when I am speaking God's message and when I am speaking only my own thoughts. Developing a fitting personal style is a lifelong quest.

My prayer is that every pastor will become a great preacher who communicates love from the pulpit. I want you to identify and appreciate the uniqueness of the church in which God has placed you. I pray for you to discover why God has sent you to this particular assignment at this period in human history.

As I travel for Focus on the Family, I am awestruck by the hundreds of faithful pastors who are determined to bring the gospel to a changing culture. They are searching for effective tools and new insights to build into ministries. I have met so many who long to do their work well. I salute you for strategizing to win people with the life-giving gospel. Perhaps these suggestions will help you keep flexible in style and changeless in substance:

*Welcome change as a friend.*
Your attitude toward change will often determine how others respond to it. Those we serve in ministry are sometimes more eager to change than we think. Some have experience in dealing with new business plans, upgraded computer systems or hostile takeovers. Don't hesitate to ask their advice about how they have been able to make change work for them. Your congregants will be pleased when you initiate such conversations and listen to the experience they share.

*Get a firm grasp on what is eternal.*
Stick to the changeless elements of the gospel with all your strength and influence. Then be willing to consider changing everything else. In many churches, people do not know the difference between the eternal and the passing, so they need your direction and steadfastness.

*Refuse to take resistance personally.*
Often what seems like resistance is fear. By talking things through openly, you may allay the worries of many. On the other hand, such a discussion may lead you to reconsider, and later you may thank God that your idea was never implemented. Sometimes your members' resistance may be God's good gift to you.

Listen to those who resist change so you may profit from their reasoning.

*Check your attitude toward change.*
Some unknown writer advised, "Change not the masses but change the fabric of your own soul and your own visions, and you change all." The most needed change may be inside us. I love to think about Henry Thoreau's short observation, "Things do not change; we change."[1]

*Mere change is not progress.*
Pushing a congregation to change just for the sake of a new program never makes them more like the Savior. I recently read a German proverb that helped shape my thinking about change: "To change and to improve are two different things."[2] How true that realization has been in my service to Christ.

The change the Church most needs is the transformation of hard hearts and empowerment of weak resolve. If you keep your eyes fixed on the Savior, you will have the backbone to change what must be changed, the freedom to allow change when it is needed and the wisdom to know what must never change.

—H. B. L.

### Notes
1. Louis E. Boone, *Quotable Business* (New York: Random House, 1992), p. 300.
2. Ibid.

# isn't it enough to be anointed?

Do you remember the Rajneesh cult that came from India to the United States?

I saw communities of this cult for the first time when I visited India in the early '80s. I could hardly stand the sight of their orgies, filled as they were with an incredible display of opulence and unbridled sexual activity. Followers dressed in various shades of red and treated their leader like a god. I wondered what kind of twisted thinking allowed a man to receive such worship, such accolades.

One day the newspapers announced that the Rajneesh cult was setting up shop in eastern Oregon. The cult members had chosen this site as their base of operations for impacting North America. Because of my experience in India, I felt apprehensive about the results of their presence in our state. I asked a lawyer friend to drive up to the community where they were setting up shop, so we could see for ourselves.

As we drove down the gravel road toward the commune, posted guards made sure we knew that we were being watched. The enormous number of persons dressed in red clothing made the scene surreal. As we drove through the area, the cult members went about business as though we did not exist. No one spoke. No one asked our names. No one inquired about what brought us to the community. We did not exist as far as they were concerned.

Soon the whole scene changed. As if responding to some secret signal, everyone moved to the roadside. As the Bhagwan

Shree Rajneesh passed by, his devotees worshiped him, as they did every afternoon when he was driven down this road in one of his more-than-100 Rolls Royces. I watched the crowds as they shouted, waved and bowed in his honor; and I thought about Jesus arriving in Jerusalem on Palm Sunday. The cult followers showered their leader with flowers. They cheered as if they were in the presence of royalty. The Bhagwan had such a regal self-image that he didn't even get out of the car. From his backseat, he simply waved to his subjects. Then the parade ended and the Rolls picked up speed and drove away. Worshipers were left to rejoice over their short glimpse of their glorious leader.

Under God's intervention, the civil authorities in Oregon concluded that the Bhagwan was unethical and that his past was tainted. His shady financial dealings were untangled, and his house of cards collapsed. He was banned from the entire state of Oregon and his followers left. Later he died, a faded image of what he had been.

As I think about the Bhagwan, I am reminded how easy it is for pastors to develop an inflated view of themselves and their work. The apostle Paul warns, "Do not think of yourself more highly than you ought, but rather think of yourself with sober judgment, in accordance with the measure of faith God has given you" (Rom. 12:3). Though we pastors have high visibility, we must resist cravings for royalty. The moment we think of ourselves too highly, we start a treacherous slide into pride. Then, being treated like a monarch becomes more important than ministry, and status more important than service.

Sometimes our views of ourselves fools us. I overheard a mature layperson say, "Our young pastor would vehemently deny wanting to be treated like a king, but he never stops anyone who does it." And one national leader, puzzled by today's Church, told me, "It no longer seems enough for ministers to be anointed; now they want to be royalty." I pray that these two comments reflect rare exceptions. Unfortunately, in some groups of pastors, I see far too many issues that seem to validate such judgments.

The temptation to idolize Christian leaders has been around since New Testament times. Paul and Barnabas were received warmly when they arrived at Lystra (see Acts 14:8-18). They experienced wonderful acceptance and great success. Through their ministry, God healed a cripple who had never walked. In the excitement, the crowd began to think these missionaries were gods. They decided to call robust Barnabas, Zeus, the Greek god of the pantheon, the ruler of the heavens and the father of other gods. They thought Paul, because of his convincing speaking ability, must be Hermes, the Greek god of eloquent rhetoric. When people threw themselves at the apostles' feet to worship them as gods, these New Testament preachers were horrified. "Get on your feet!" they exclaimed. "We are only men like you."

Paul did not enjoy that kind of praise. Instead, he used their false assumptions to teach them that the apostles had come to introduce them to the living God. As people in many other settings have done since, these hearers tried to fit the message of Christ into their cultural patterns. As a result, they never fully heard the true gospel. If we allow our hearers to worship us, we do them a great disservice. They will end up worshiping the messenger instead of the One who sent us, and they will never feel obliged to apply Christ's message to their lives. The best thing a pastor can do to avoid falling into this trap is to cultivate an attitude of humility. Only insofar as God works through us can we truly bless those around us. In a contemporary thought pattern, Eugene H. Peterson paraphrases the words of Paul and Barnabas: "We're not gods! We are men just like you, and we're here to bring you the Message, to persuade you to abandon these silly god-superstitions and embrace God himself, the living God. We don't make God; he makes us, and all of this—sky, earth, sea, and everything in them" (Acts 14:15, *THE MESSAGE*).

Perhaps there is an important lesson for us from the short life of the hero worship in this passage. Soon after Paul and Barnabas made this speech forbidding their followers to worship them, Jews came from Antioch and Iconium, won the crowd over and stoned the preachers. They even dragged poor Paul out of the city, thinking he was dead. The next day Paul and Barnabas left for Derbe. Hero worship soon brought them a stoning.

How does all of this relate to today's pastors? I worry a lot about ministers who so hunger for prominence that they will do almost anything to get it. In fact, some pastors believe they have rights to special treatment because of their assignments or their success. We would do well to follow Paul and Barnabas's example and to hold lightly to those moments of man-made victory and recognition.

Let's understand the essential foundations of ministry. In the final analysis, pastors have no rights. Our future is in God's hands—a good place to be. Everything we have is a gift from God. We owe Him grateful thanks for the blessings, mercies and potentialities He places in our hands. And we are more likely to find balance in ministry when we admit to God that the great opportunity He has given us calls for our best effort and our greatest commitment.

An addictive craving for ministerial royalty gives the Church a bad case of "heart" trouble. I am always disappointed when a pastor expects favored status. I feel alarmed when ministers manipulate perks, raises and status at the expense of sacrificial giving of little people. It worries me when ministry colleagues appear more concerned about the size of their home or the model of their car than about seeing themselves as missionaries in a pagan world. "Superstar" and "pastor" are words that don't fit in the same sentence. Nor can they coexist in the heart of an undershepherd of Christ.

Let's face facts. Many pastors experience upward social mobility because of ministry perks. There is nothing wrong with living well when congregations are able to support us generously. We should be worthy of our hire. But their generous care doesn't mean that we have a right to it or that we should be greedy for more. If we allow houses, cars and status to become more important to us than the salvation of the lost—more important to us than the care of our Lord's bewildered sheep—then our priorities need serious adjustment.

Colleagues in ministry, I say this to you as I say it to myself: You have been providentially placed in a pagan world to serve as missionaries for Christ. The moment we see ourselves as anything but missionaries to this culture, we become driven by paychecks and status. So many high-profile colleagues have fallen from grace in full view of the Church and the watching world. Often these pastors became so used to superstar status that they will not settle for less.

The call of God on your life makes you a child of the King. Rejoice in that reality. As sons and daughters of God, we enjoy miraculous benefits and amazing assignments, but we are not the King. And we will never be the King.

The King—almighty God—trusts us with a portion of His Church. We preach from the King's pulpit. We work in the King's office. We represent the King many times every day. We serve the King's people. We speak for the King. We oversee the King's Church. We care for the King's flocks. But we are not the King. Thus we possess no right to set ourselves up as someone to be exalted or pampered. We have been given great opportunities to represent our King. Let's do it with the anointing. Turn the applause His way. Give Him the glory.

If you sometimes have a craving for royalty, what are the remedies?

*Evaluate your desire for prominence.*

God's verdict on power abusers is tough. He refuses to keep company with those who practice expediency and moral shortcuts. But He takes joy in empowering the weak, energizing the weary and enriching the humble.

*Take on the spirit of a servant.*

A pastor in our town was afraid he was losing the servant's touch, so he volunteered to serve a half day per week in a shelter for homeless people. He refused to give the director his full name. He said he wanted to be sure he was a true servant. I imagine his sermons were full of grace every Sunday after serving at the shelter, don't you?

*Take a walk around the church.*

Look at the pulpit. Thank the Lord for letting you use it. Do the same with your study, your car, your books and your privileges or perks that come with your ministry. Get out the membership list of your church and thank God for each person He allows you to serve in His name.

*Clarify your perspective on anointing and royalty.*

God promises to anoint the preacher, not because He has to do it, but because He wants our ministry to be effective. The anointing is a holy, supernatural gift, given to be useful, not to be put on display. The anointing turns the human preaching effort into a love gift to

Christ. On the other hand, those who seek royalty believe they have rights and that somebody owes them something. I recently heard a Christian worker remark, "We have paid our dues and the church owes us something for all our years of service." I wonder where that false notion started. I don't think the rumor began at the foot of the Cross.

If you seek royalty, you will discover, like any addict, only an unquenchable thirst for more privileges and honors. But if you seek anointing, you will find that your thirst for power will be replaced by a thirst for God. Both you and your church will be refreshed.

—H. B. L.

# you matter to me

How could I have missed the signs?

I cohosted a TV program with a pastoral colleague for seven years in a major TV market in the Northwest. Our telecast was sandwiched between Jerry Falwell and Oral Roberts in a popular time slot on Sunday mornings. Our program was aired on a commercial channel, so many unchurched persons watched before they switched to the Sunday-morning news programs.

My colleague on the program was a gifted and well-educated minister. He was handsome, articulate, scintillating and bright. We developed a wonderful friendship during those daylong TV tapings, since we normally did three or four programs at a time to be aired over subsequent weeks. I looked forward to those times in the studio. The ministry we shared was an adventure in communicating the good news and had a positive impact on many people.

While we worked together, we talked about ministry and about family, as good friends do. What my friend never told me was that he was involved with a woman who was not his wife. One day the phone rang, and I received news that his affair had been exposed. He was leaving his church at the insistence of its leadership. His ministry had been morally compromised. I was shocked, sad, angry and guilty. Another minister had fallen prey to the enemy.

A fallen minister lives the rest of life with a sad spirit of remorse and regret. Many who have experienced sexual ship-wreck tell me they never live a full day when the question of what might have been does not haunt their thoughts. That's pain, big-time. I share this story to encourage every pastor to keep moral-ly pure and to scrupulously avoid even an appearance of evil. Usually pastors react to the moral failures among their fellow pastors by expressing regret and moving on. Occasionally we stop to make mental note of the fact that we might be in the same predicament save for the grace of God. But can't we do more? What can we do to help avert these failures in others? The pressing question is how we can help others before they commit immoral acts that lead to a life of guilt and shame.

When I heard about my friend, I asked myself: *How could I have helped? Could I have known about his weakness and temptations? If I had known, would I have been able to intervene in such a private mat-ter?*

What needs to change so that colleagues in Christian min-istry do more than make small talk when they meet? Somehow we must think creatively about taking more responsibility for one another. In any relationship, someone has to puncture the shell of shallow communication about weather, civic matters, children and routine ministry. Someone has to ask tough ques-tions. And someone has to ask about our relationship to Jesus.

I feel terrible about my fallen TV cohost. Years have passed, and he has become very successful in another field. But in look-ing back, I realize that our relationship stayed on such a super-ficial level that I never had a chance to stand in his way and say, "Are you sure you want to go this way? Have you thought of the pain you will cause your family and yourself? Do you really want what you are about to buy?"

When I hear of other fallen ministers, I wonder if others could have known enough about their struggles to have gotten in their faces and said, "Stop this foolishness." Sometimes when I see a wonderful ministry couple destroyed, I ask God, "Why didn't I take them into my arms and prayed with such love, compassion and intensity that they would have abandoned their course to brokenness?"

Am I the only one to whom the Spirit of God is saying, "You have to do something"? I think not. I don't have any easy answers. But I do have some sense of what to say and how to say it. However, before I say something, I need to know about their temptations. Danger lurks around every corner for every pastor. Maybe we should make a commitment of loving responsibility to ask one another: "How are things going at home? Is your activity on the Internet giving you access to unwholesome materials? Are you faithfully giving yourself to developing a quality marriage? And how would your spouse answer the same questions?"

I celebrate the new emphasis among pastors today to find soul friends and to establish prayer partners. Neil and I have emphasized this principle in every book we have written. In establishing such relationships of voluntary accountability, we must give our prayer-partner colleague permission to ask us about our motives, marriage and ministry. But what about those hundreds of pastors who most need accountability and never seek it?

I really believe we must become actively responsible for one another. For the sake of the Church, we can no longer tolerate brothers and sisters falling by the wayside because of a careless act or an unbridled emotion. Too many tragedies are weakening the Church and bringing shame to Christ's name. Too many fine pastors are lost from the ministry workforce because of a stupid fling. Too many of our fellow pastors are setting themselves up for lifelong regret.

I propose we become much more proactive. When we see colleagues struggling, what stops us from going to them? Don't be so polite and so discreet that you allow a friend to walk over the precipice of moral failure into ministerial oblivion. Take the risk. See if a kind word or even a strong warning could save that friend's ministry. Just think how many colleagues have invalidated their ministries because of poor decisions, idiotic relationships or blatant sins. Could we have stopped them if we had known when to speak up?

Let's take more responsibility for colleagues and tell them, "Stop!" Here are a few suggestions:

*Give attention to the brightest.*
Every human being faces temptation of some sort, regardless of talent or age, and many find sexual temptations the most difficult to resist. In addition, for some unknown reason, the brightest and most gifted pastors are among those who are most likely to fall morally and spiritually. Perhaps they cannot deal with all the marvelous gifts they have been given or perhaps their giftedness tempts them to rely on themselves more than on God. At any rate, someone needs to take responsibility for them. These bright folks may seem intimidating to some, but don't forget that however bright or talented they are, they still need friends who love them enough to confront them and to pray them through temptation.

*Offer to become a soul friend.*
Whatever you call the relationship—soul friend, mentor, prayer partner—offer to be an accountability partner with another pastor. They may not accept, but they might be pleased by your offer. If such a relationship is to produce maximum effectiveness, permission must be given to ask tough questions.

*Develop spiritual sensitivities.*

Some pastors possess a holy ESP system and can sense problems before anyone else has an inkling that anything may be wrong. Maybe this insight should be called a moral early-warning system. At any rate, develop and use your sensitivities to show you when you need to speak to a colleague about these issues.

A pastor's wife from the last generation called it "spiritual cat whiskers." Pastors must keep their spiritual antennae turned to the On position. Not every one of us has this special gift, but all of us can train ourselves to ask, "How are things going at home?" or "Tell me about your prayer life," or "Bring me up to date on what your spouse thinks about your ministry."

*Become proactive.*

I dream of a situation in which pastors will start saying to each other, *Since much of our culture seems to be in a moral sewer, I have promised God I would ask every pastor I meet, "How is it with your soul? How are you doing spiritually and morally?"* Of course, someone bent on hiding sin will not wish for such closeness, but their refusal of close relationships should be a good reason to stay especially close to them.

*Reach out to hurting clergy couples.*

To create an atmosphere in which a couple can open up and share their deep concerns takes time and energy on the part of the pastor/mentor. If you wish to maintain the purity of the Church, you will need to accept the challenge that every hurting clergy couple needs someone to accept and value them. Ask God which ministry

couples need you the most, and then give something of
yourself to them in supportive affirmation. Hurting
couples are not hard to spot in community ministerial
associations or in other pastoral gatherings. Of course,
the serendipity of service is such that when we reach out
to help others, we are surprised again to see that God has
decided to help us as well.

—H. B. L.

# revival at the grass roots

Confusion abounds these days about revival. It is hard to know if such confusion is due to the meaning of the word or to an anxiety that something so sweeping and so spiritual might change us, our churches and our culture forever.

It is fair for you to ask me what I mean when I use the word "revival." Am I speaking of a spiritual breakthrough in a single congregation? Spiritual renewal of an individual? A sweeping, historical event with cataclysmic impact on society, like the great awakenings of history? As for me, I would be delighted to experience revival in any or all of the above forms—personal, church or society.

Obviously, our period in history is experiencing spiritual decay, moral pollution and the declining influence of the Church. Yet our bookstores overflow with books discussing spirituality. As believers engage in endless word games about revival, our churches and our world are confused and are drawn to a spirituality that worships self and stuff. These days we need a supernatural, spiritual transformation more than ever before.

Years ago I was profoundly influenced by two paragraphs written by J. B. Chapman, a beloved leader from my denomination's past. His longing for revival in his time sounds like the hunger I feel and hear expressed today. I have intentionally withheld Chapman's dates, because I do not want anyone to skip over these timeless sentences, which have been edited only slightly. About revival, Chapman wrote:

> The revival I seek is not the product of the labors of some personality-plus evangelist. Such a revival is too detached and impersonal to meet my needs or to answer my prayers. I want that kind of revival that comes in spite of the singing, the preaching, the testimonies, and the human attractions or detractions. I want that kind of revival because it takes that kind to really revive me.[1]

Catch the intensity of the hunger of his soul as Chapman continues:

> I want a revival that, like a summer shower, will purify the atmosphere of our churches everywhere, and which will awaken the dormant forces of our people young and old. I want something so general and so divine that it will be uncontrollable. I want something that will reemphasize old-time moral and spiritual values. Something that will reform and regenerate down and out sinners and save respectable worldlings. Something that will bring in the youth and the little children. Something so attractive that it will break over into the circles of the pleasure-loving. Something that will set people on their back tracks to make restitution for wrongs committed. Something that will bring God to bear upon cultural problems like divorce and racism. Something that will inject old-time honesty, veracity, and purity, and other-world-mindedness in our preachers and people. Something that will make the namby-pamby, soft-

handed, compromising, cringing sort of Christianity as obsolete as Phariseeism was on the day of Pentecost. Something that reveals a minister's credentials by souls saved and established in Jesus Christ.[2]

Authentic revival enables a congregation to be transformed from a barely making-it church to an unbelievable supernatural, powerhouse of achievement. It brings refreshment, renewal and anointing, which cause a church to become an amazing force for righteousness, energized by God. Revival often starts from a holy desperation of a pastor or laity for a church to be changed and renewed.

Revival stirs a congregation so it becomes eager to get on track spiritually. Revival empowers clergy and other church leaders to live radical Christianity in every dimension of their living—inside and outside the church. Consider the incredible benefits a revival provides for a congregation:

*Spiritual normalcy is restored.*
Revival takes a church forward to its basic purposes, making it healthy, robust and redemptive. Since revival requires restitution, forgiveness and reordering of priorities, it helps believers refocus their commitments to God and to His work in the world. Revival increases dependence on prayer, worship, witness and service. When revival restores spiritual normalcy to a congregation, the church becomes much more than a feeble imitation of a garden club, a service organization or a well-intentioned welfare provider. The renewed church becomes an army of Christ-saturated people whose weapons are love, faith and hope.

No one can fully explain the amazing changes revival brings. A revival makes a church different even though it has the same pastor, songs, meeting time, worshipers and facility. The real secret is that holy living becomes the natural practice of the people of God. Then the church fulfills her spiritual mission much like the Early Church in the book of Acts.

*Extraordinary prayer is activated.*
No one knows whether prayer brings revival or revival stirs new interest in prayer. Although we cannot fully understand the mystery of revival, both the Bible and church history teach us a significant component is prayer. No prayer—no revival.

There are about 365,000 Christian congregations in the United States. What if only 50 percent of them had a three-month emphasis on prayer? Although some who attend these churches know little about prayer, many are interested. Teach and preach about prayer. Organize prayer watches and prayer summits. Provide prayer seminars and prayer walks. Above everything else, get people together to learn to pray. It is the single most important component of the revival we seek from God.

*Sin is feared.*
Spiritual cancer is spreading everywhere in our society. It is attacking homes, schools, churches and government. Listen to the TV talk shows or read the front pages of the nation's newspapers. A holy cure is needed immediately. Revival forces us to face sin and the damaging consequences. Like cancer, sin requires radical

surgery if a person or church is to regain spiritual health.

Other effects of sin are devastating, too. Worse than the effects of the dreaded sin cancer in an individual is the not-so-obvious damage brought on a congregation by corporate sin. Although we may not feel comfortable thinking about it, many churches are anemic, handicapped, feeble and too weak for spiritual combat because of known or unknown, inner or outer, and "respectable" or vile sins in our fellowships. The long-range consequences of these congregational sins cripple a church for generations. Personal and/or congregational sin must be acknowledged, forgiven, forsaken and cleansed.

*The supernatural is welcomed.*
Remember Peter, the spiritual coward before Pentecost, to whom the Holy Spirit gave such boldness? After Acts 4:29,30, Peter prayed for miraculous results so that the Early Church could convince doubters who were watching from the outside, as well as strengthen the faith of believers on the inside. God answered Peter's prayer by giving him incredible courage to speak for God. The Lord also gave the congregation unity of purpose, generosity to others and power to outlive their enemies.

*Love becomes magnetic.*
When an authentic revival takes place in a church, believers begin treating others as they would treat Christ. The golden rule starts to work spontaneously. Believers confess sin, request and grant forgiveness, repair relationships and make restitution for wrongs.

One says, "I'm sorry," while another says, "It's okay; I should have grown past our disagreement months ago."

Renewed love at church automatically spreads like a holy epidemic to offices, factories, gas stations, convenience stores, schools, Fortune 500 companies—wherever Christ-lovers find themselves. This holy love flowing through Christians to unbelievers becomes a powerful force for evangelism. Even though the spiritually needy usually cannot be scolded out of their sins or reasoned into the Kingdom, they can be loved to Jesus.

In the renewal of love brought about in revival, the believers' witness becomes attractive and natural. It shows on the tennis court, on the golf course, in shopping malls, in family rooms, in PTA meetings and anywhere else we meet people who need the Savior. Outsiders who feel that love are drawn to attend church. Often, they come back again and again to bask in the love of God flowing through a Christ-exalting church.

Let's consider Charles Spurgeon's insightful advice about revivals:

If you want to move a train, you don't need a new engine, or even ten engines—you need to light a fire and get the steam up in the engine you now have. It is not a new person or a new plan, but the life of God in them that the church needs. Let us ask God for it! Perhaps God is ready to shake the world at its very foundations. Perhaps even now He is about to pour forth a mighty influence upon His people which shall make the church in this age as vital as it ever was in any age that has passed.[3]

Light the fire and get up steam for the engines and pray, "O Lord, revive Thy work in me!" If you long for revival, remember it requires tending and strengthening the soul of your church.

—N. B. W.

### Notes

1. Neil B. Wiseman, ed., *Evangelism: 139 Ideas and Quotes* (Kansas City, MO: Beacon Hill Press, 1983), back cover.
2. Ibid.
3. Richard J. Foster and James Bryan Smith, eds., *Devotional Classics* (San Francisco: HarperSanFrancisco, 1993), p. 335.

# the grief of leaving

When you love your congregation, it is hard to move on. I have never had more pain than when I have left a church. Leaving people I love has been among the most agonizing emotional experiences I have ever had. When the day comes when it's time to leave, you need more courage than you can muster by yourself.

Let's face realities. Ministers come and go. Sometimes we realize our work is done in a place. Maybe a forced resignation makes leaving compulsory. Sometimes an inner voice tells us it is right to accept a different assignment. But whatever the reason, leaving creates sorrow for the pastor, the family and the church.

I began my ministry in a little church on the wrong side of the tracks when I was 23. I remember walking into that place for the first time. The property was beat up and so were the people. No need to talk about class—there was none. Still, I remember loving those people and serving them. They loved me back, and their love taught me so much about what is important in ministry. Those wonderful people accepted me and allowed me room to grow. God blessed the congregation and it grew, forcing us to build a new church building. After three and a half years, I moved to another assignment in California and then on to Salem, Oregon, where I stayed for nearly 20 years. I completed my pastoral service in Pasadena, California, in 1991, but I felt the same horrible pain every time I left a church.

Pastoral ministry brings tough times and good times. I have served loving people and some who were difficult to love. You probably have a few members from each of these groups in your present parish. But no matter who was in my church, my assignment was ministry all the way—Christ was exalted, and I was fulfilled.

Then my cousin Dr. James Dobson and I started talking about how Focus on the Family could expand its efforts to hurting pastors and their families. Focus had a long record of coming alongside clergy, but an experienced pastor was needed to give this aspect of their ministry a clearer direction.

Let me tell you about one of my low times during this period of deliberation. The decision had been made to resign my pastorate. Beverley and I flew to Colorado Springs and stayed in a hotel while we worked out adjusting finances, locating a house, leaving family and being without a congregation. I sat in our hotel room looking out at Pikes Peak and crying like a baby. Though I was sure the decision was right, I understood that I would never forget this pain.

My message to you is this—ministry, by definition, creates such an intimate bond of Christian love between pastor and congregation that leaving a church can cause almost as much grief as losing an old friend. Though the new assignment brings new relationships, those friendships do not wipe out the heartache we have over losing what was. Though it's healthy to admit such a sense of loss, you must also find ways to work through it. It's especially important to help your family work through their grief over parting. Don't forget to make allowance for the mourning. The church people you are leaving often feel rejected, sad and hurt. In fact, some church members act out their frustrations in negative behaviors and destructive attitudes you may find hard to understand.

Here are several strategies to help you deal with the pain caused by leaving a church:

*Use your grief skills.*
As an experienced pastor, think back on ways you helped people deal with loss in their lives. Remember how grief washes over one like waves—in the midst of apparent calm, a great breaker appears from nowhere.

*Tell God your feelings.*
Tell the Father in your prayers how confused you are about leaving and starting again. Ask Him why you feel such a sense of loss when you are sure He has directed you to your new assignment. The dialogue will strengthen you.

*Connections are imprinted on your soul.*
Admit the reality of the ties you have with your old church and manage those connections wisely. Think about how you can cherish memories without creating problems for the new pastor. When you minister to a family in its darkest hours, you should not expect to get over it. And neither will they. Though relationships change, these significant ministry ties cannot be broken or forgotten. Nor should they be.

*Listen to spiritually mature friends and advisors.*
Neil tells of the lessons he learned from Mrs. Howell when he moved from his first church. He was young and green, but his heart was in the right place. To help the new pastor's start-up, Neil told his congregation that they needed to love the new pastor intentionally. So far, so good. Then he advised his congregation that there were to be no phone calls, letters or Christmas cards. Six months after the Wisemans left, their first child was

born. A few days after Todd's birth, Mrs. Howell wrote
the baby his first letter and said, "Your daddy told us not
to write him, but he didn't tell us not to write you. I
heard that your name is Todd, and I wonder if you could
tell me how your mother and father are doing in their
new assignment." Those who have lived for a few years
have a lot to teach us if we are ready to learn.

*Use your grief to make you a better pastor.*
Thomas Jefferson's insightful quote teaches us how grief
can help us: "Grief drives men to the habits of serious
reflection, sharpens the understanding and softens the
heart."[1] Sounds like good advice for a pastor who hates
leaving.

*Don't let grief hinder you from loving the new congregation.*
Some of them feel a sense of loss for the pastor who just
left. Some of these good people are stretching to accept
you. Don't betray their fledgling trust in you by making
them feel that they can't measure up to the wonderful
church you left behind. They have loved and lost just like
you. Open your heart to the new congregation. Let them
see your love in action as new relationships are established.

—H. B. L.

**Note**
1. Hannah Ward and Jennifer Wild, comps., *The Doubleday Christian Quotation
Collection* (New York: Doubleday, 1997), p. 175.

# the Counselor

who cares

and

confronts

SECTION 2

# people—the church's reason for being

Charlie—not his real name—called himself our sanitary engineer, but he was really the church janitor. Give him any title you want, but he was the one who cleaned the church and often caused lots of trouble. From a clean-and-orderly point of view, he did his work well; but people frustrated him so much that he would have been happier cleaning a hermit's cave. That's why his job at church got on his nerves. Human beings were his problem. From Charlie's perspective, the church would have been a perfect place without people. They dropped paper, left fingerprints and tracked in dirt. As a result, Charlie always wanted me as pastor to tell the congregation to keep the church clean and picked up.

And you can imagine how Charlie made others feel about him.

Once he pushed me so hard that I discussed his concerns with the church board. To my surprise, nearly half agreed with Charlie and said, "Our pastor should make a statement about this problem from the pulpit." I was confused. I thought churches were made for people and that we should expect them to sometimes leave the facilities in disarray. As a matter of fact, as I thought about it more, it dawned on me that churches were not just made for people. The church is people. But sometimes pastors share Charlie's attitude: the church would be great if only it were not made up of people.

Let's remember that Jess, Mary, Tony and Erica are the reason the church exists. Mrs. Carter, Mr. Jengling and Susie Mae are also part of the fellowship. Meeting human needs or providing a product is what helps businesses make a profit and defines the purpose of every profession. Newspapers exist for readers. TV channels must have viewers. Computer manufacturers serve customers. Governments depend on citizens. Schools need children. Airlines rely on travelers. Physicians care for patients.

It's true for us as pastors, as well. Without human beings, a church is superfluous. Churches must have prospects, converts and members. Without them, there would be no need to preach, pray, study and serve. Every Kingdom effort is intended to help someone.

It's easy to become so engaged in the mechanics of ministry that the reason for it all is overlooked. Charlie forgot that his job depended on human beings using the church building. Let's celebrate the fact that people are every church's most precious possession. When you evaluate the purpose of any aspect of a church's ministry, you always come back to the people.

For decades, church-growth and outreach literature has emphasized "growing" great churches. But let's sharpen the focus a bit. According to Scripture and sound logic, if we build great people, great churches will be automatic.

Some modern pastors seem willing to abandon the common touch with people. But it's a mistake to give up cultivating relationships by not loving people, caring for them or knowing them. Perhaps today's ideal of privacy has encouraged this fear of being close. Or maybe some ministers consider the people of God like customers who come during business hours to buy advertised items at the best prices in the least amount of time.

However, if we want to make our churches people friendly as the Lord intended, why not use the metaphor of family to shape them? Use the pattern of an extended two- or three-generation family in which everyone really cares for each other. Then all members are brothers and sisters, Jesus Christ is our older Brother, God is our Father, and the devil is no kin. And like any human family, a church sometimes includes a few odd fellows and one or two peculiar old ladies. Such a relational congregation draws its direction from apostle Peter's description of the Church: "But you are a chosen people, a royal priesthood, a holy nation, a people belonging to God, that you may declare the praises of him who called you out of darkness into his wonderful light" (1 Pet. 2:9). Note the relationship elements he includes, such as priesthood, nation and people. That kind of church will attract people because many folks are homesick for God and hungry for closeness with other human beings.

Such a vital congregation is made up of members of God's family who have experienced life together. They have found grace to be sufficient through one another's cancers, separations and deaths. They demonstrate that an authentic relational church consists of believers committed to bearing fruits of righteousness. They have cooked meals together for the homeless or worked to develop a prison ministry. These brothers and sisters cherish, care, sacrifice and suffer together. These are the family of God who bury their loved ones from the church as they give witness to the Resurrection in the midst of their tears and grief.

I have an old pastor friend who loved to preach, "Through those church doors walk some of the best people you will ever know. They love you. They overlook your faults. They expect to see you in heaven." He is right, and we must always remember it.

Milo Arnold, a wonderfully effective pastor from the last generation and a minister I followed in a small-town pastorate, explained it this way:

A pastor is not making discoveries in a test tube nor exploring the wonders of decaying dust. The minister is adventuring into the deep recesses of a human soul and probing the mysteries of persons who shall never cease to be. He is not building a cathedral which stands in dignity among other buildings but a person who stands in dignity before God Himself. The minister does not give people things to live with but a meaning to live for. He does not place in their hands a tool for their convenience but in their hearts an aspiration toward God.[1]

That's the kind of minister I want to be.

How can you make your church more like the family of God? How can you accept people with their weaknesses and their strengths?

*People need love.*

Even though some folks seem hard to love, everyone needs unconditional love. Let's admit that some individuals bring their problems to church with them. Others cause problems so often that one pastor jokingly remarked, "The main reason sheep exist is to complicate the life of the shepherd." But another minister replied in their defense, "That's the nature of sheep." Whatever the cause of their problems—injured, crippled, limping, abused—sheep need a shepherd to help them find healing and hope.

Some folks have become spiritually deformed by years of gospel sterility and shriveled love. They feel abused, with good cause, by wrongs done to them in the name of righteousness, by unresolved conflicts and by hurts from unfair gossip. They feel beat up from too many pastoral changes, and they feel anguish from adult children abandoning the church. Those dear ones need someone like us to really care for them with a love like Eugene Peterson describes: "Love enables the eyes to see what has been there all along but was overlooked in haste or indifference. Love corrects stigmatism [*sic*] so that what was distorted in selfishness is not perceived accurately and appreciatively. Love cures shortsightedness so that the blue of the distant other is now in wondrous focus."[2]

*People come before institutions.*
If human needs conflict with institutional priorities, human beings must come first—no question. While most of us really believe this concept, we may not always practice it. Our priority is to build great Christians.

*People are a church's most valuable possession.*
Wayne Dosick, a secular business writer, says, "When you give your people what they need—including the time to rest and rejuvenate, restore and renew—they will return your investment in ample measure, helping you to achieve greater and greater yield from your business."[3] What Dosick says about business is even more important for a church. People are to be served, not used; motivated, not manipulated; loved, not abused.

*People need acceptance.*
A church will help believers and new people feel accepted when it is a place
    —to find strength for daily struggles
    —to connect with trustworthy people
    —to receive and give love
    —to provide opportunities for service

—to find vital faith for contemporary living
—to be challenged to be more Christlike

*People bring satisfaction.*
What joy pastors feel when seekers come to Christ for forgiveness of sins. What satisfaction we experience when persons mature in Christ under our spiritual care. What delight we enjoy when they perform acts of courageous selflessness and show symptoms of deepening commitment. The years have taught me that memories of serving together in the local church are among the greatest blessings pastors ever experiences.

*People are hungry to know God.*
These days millions of spiritually empty secularists are searching for meaning. Listen to TV. Read national magazines. Check out the self-help and New Age sections of bookstores. The reality is as obvious as the morning sun—many are searching for God, but they are looking in the wrong places. Many of these hungry folks never consider church because they have heard it is rigid, old-fashioned and irrelevant. They don't realize what a connectedness they might discover there. Dale Galloway's and George Hunter's books are helping us learn to use language secularists understand. Though some newer strategies for reaching the unchurched may seem somewhat revolutionary, the message is as old as the Bible— love people to Christ.

My own way of keeping focused on people is rooted in an inspiring portion of Scripture. After an attempted retreat with His disciples, Jesus is interrupted by a hungry crowd of five thousand. Mark records our Master's reaction: "When Jesus landed [in a boat] and saw a large crowd, he had compassion on them, because they were like sheep without a shepherd. So he began teaching them many things" (Mark 6:34). Those haunting words—"They were like sheep without a shepherd"—put my passion for ministry into high gear.

When we evangelize or develop discipleship programs, our challenge is to focus on people. They are the reason Jesus died. Since He loved them that much, surely we must serve them gladly. They are the reason the Church exists. The Lord calls us to serve them—with their warts, idiosyncrasies, potential and possibilities.

—N. B. W.

### Notes

1. Milo Arnold, *The Adventure of the Christian Ministry* (Kansas City, MO: Beacon Hill Press, 1967), p. 18.
2. Eugene Peterson, *Living the Message* (San Francisco: Harper, 1996), p. 46.
3. Wayne Dosick, *The Business Bible* (New York: HarperBusiness, 1993), p. 147.

# treasures in
# broken vessels

God uses unmistakable moments to put us in the right place at the right time to accomplish His plan for someone. Sometimes we are surprised, even amazed. A living example of this heads an inner-city mission in the Northwest. For more than a decade, my friend has cared for the underprivileged, transients, unwed mothers, homeless families and dysfunctional persons who come and go through the community. He leads an effective ministry to hurting people, and I greatly admire him for what he does.

He was not always this way, however. Once he was a struggling alcoholic. This, along with other addictions, nearly destroyed him. He felt alone and sincerely believed he had been victimized by the world around him. Then one day, he turned to our congregation, who accepted and cared for him.

But I am getting ahead of my story. Let me tell you how our relationship became a "God thing."

My part in the story started when the phone rang at two o'clock in the morning. I listened sleepily as a police officer told me that a man was asking for me from his jail cell. I reminded myself of my promise to God many years before that I would go wherever anyone needed me. I dressed, tiptoed from the bedroom and left for the jail as quickly as I could. When I arrived, I found a broken man, arrested for a crime he had committed years earlier.

It was not my role to lord it over this man, regardless of his sin, mistakes or present situation. Nor was it my place to present myself as a superspiritual person who would throw Scriptures at him. I would not use my position as pastor to give an impression that I spoke for God. I had been learning for years to believe contacts like this are a special privilege, ordered by the Lord. Once again, I would have the honor of loving someone in pain and assuring him that God loved him, too. As an extension of that love, my church would also stand beside him. From my perspective, that response is an automatic part of our admonition to be Christlike.

Soon after I arrived at the jail and during our conversation, he surrendered his life to Jesus and became a Christian. From that time forward, this man blossomed and grew spiritually. After he was released from jail, he volunteered at the inner-city mission. Later, he married a loving wife and accepted added responsibilities. Ultimately, he became the director of the inner-city work, which has flourished under his leadership.

I wonder what might have happened if I had stayed in bed that night, excusing myself as too tired to go. What if I had called the jail chaplain to make the contact? And what might have happened if our church had not been open, loving and responsive to him?

And what effect would it have had on me and on my church if I had simply passed him on to someone else? How would I have handled the lost opportunity, emotionally and spiritually? We would all have missed so much joy in this situation had we let someone else do our work. Pastors who only want to deal with comfortable and convenient situations don't realize what they miss.

Let me share another example of a surprising call for help. One day a friend of mine stopped to help a woman with a broken-down car stalled on an off-ramp at one of the busy freeways in the Pasadena, California, area. My friend could tell this woman was different because of her seductive clothing and her multicolored hair. He concluded that she was a prostitute. The lady seemed less worried about her car than about her drug problem and her loneliness. She worried at how angry her pimp would be for this loss of her time and how much money she would lose because of this delay. She went on and on. My friend had never seen or heard anything like it. He didn't know what to do; but he thought somebody should do something, so he told her, "I have a friend who will be able to help you." Only a short time later, my friend and this woman walked into my office at the church.

You can imagine the curiosity that spread throughout the administrative wing as staff and workers came out of their offices to see who H. B. was talking to. No one could remember seeing a real-live hooker in our church.

She told me her sad story. Her tears carried mascara traces down her cheeks in little rivers that dropped to the carpet. Though I was taken aback, I found myself saying, "Well, I know my friend Jesus. He loves you even though you might not think He does. If you will give Him an opportunity, He can transform your life. Would you like to accept Jesus?"

Her answer was yes.

She didn't ask who Jesus was or what He would do for her. She didn't say she had been religious before. She just said, "Yes."

That day Christ walked into her troubled life. In a wonderful, mysterious moment, she accepted Jesus as Savior and began an exciting transformation. What followed was the hard part. It was difficult for Mary to walk away from everything she knew—the money, her support system, the old life and the few friends she had in her miserable world. Even though her pimp was vicious and mean, he was her protector. Think of the confusion she experienced when she came to church. She'd sit near the back, and many church folks were afraid of her. Her short skirts, her multicolored hair and her overdone makeup made it difficult for the Body of Christ to accept her.

As she worked at her new faith, she would come to my office to talk about her loneliness and discuss the battles she was fighting with drugs. She told me how difficult it was to make new friends. I tried to tell her about the love of God. I told her that the change would take time and be difficult. I told her that if she would hang on, she would make it; but sadly, she lost the battle.

The last time I saw Mary, she was standing on a street corner on Colorado Boulevard in Pasadena waiting for the next trick to come her way.

Since then, I've wondered what I did wrong or what I failed to do. I've often wondered where Mary is today or if she is even alive. I know she made her own choices, but I wondered if we had given her the help and acceptance she needed to help her make the right choices. I wondered what I might have done differently. I wondered how the church might have done more.

I know the ministry to down-and-outers is not easy; but it's right, though it may not be effective every time. If the Church wants to honor her Lord in reaching out to the lost, she must not only help them to know the saving, loving knowledge of Jesus Christ. She must also nurture them, care for them, disciple them, lead them and introduce them to Christians who will help them find their way. That's why they call you pastor—because you care.

Perhaps it is the lack of real compassion that gives rise to the surprising fact that George Barna discovered in his research: the average new Christian lasts for only eight weeks in today's local church. That statistic broke my heart. I'm sure it breaks yours as well.

What do these stories have to do with each other? Why would anybody have convicts and prostitutes on their prospect list? And others might say, "H. B., we don't want that kind of people in our church. Other churches can handle these cases better than we can."

These stories show we win some and lose some. However, when people do turn to Christ, we must not feel satisfied that our job is done. The Great Commission has two sides—winning sinners and helping converts discover the joy of living like Christ. Evangelism and nurture are two sides of the task of pointing the spiritually needy to the Savior. Let me suggest ways you can make it work more effectively in the congregation you serve:

*Live the gospel.*
Live out the "whosoever will" (Matt. 16:25; 20:27; Mark 8:34, *KJV*) of the gospel. Try winning someone to Christ who is outside your social comfort zone. If you are pastor of a middle-class church, you may have to model for your members the desire to win those who are at the front lines of despairing and who are lost, broken and confused, whether they are from a lower or higher social class. You will be surprised what spiritual vitality enters your church when you have a wide cultural variety. Ask God to keep you and your church from limiting your evangelism to winning only one kind of people.

*Keep near the action.*
Never allow yourself to personally turn away from all frontline evangelism. As your church grows and you add staff, you may be tempted to turn evangelism over to a specialist. Now I am not suggesting that you avoid having a gifted evangelist on staff. But keep your own heart

tender and your call fresh, by working with spiritually needy individuals. You will never regret knowing first-hand the miracles of redemption God is doing through your church.

*See potential.*

When I first met that broken man in his prison cell, I had no idea about how useful he would be for the Kingdom. On the contrary, no one knows what an influence for God Mary might have been. Every person we meet has great potential for God. Ask Him to help you see everyone as He sees them.

*Real shepherds cannot ignore cries for help.*

As the church grows and its ministry becomes more specialized, the pastor may not be able to be involved in the lives of every potential convert. But to fulfill our call to ministry and to be like the Lord who called us, we must personally answer enough of those cries for help that we get our hands dirty and our hearts broken by hurting people. If you have decided to become a church CEO or a ranch manager, you may never experience the soul-shaping, spiritual adventure I discovered in ministry to that prisoner and that prostitute. Please reconsider your decision.

*Check the cornerstone of commitment.*

Almost every minister I know first felt called to save souls. John Wesley taught that saving souls was our main business. Renew that personal commitment to winning lost people and challenge your congregation to join you. Hardly a problem in your church would not be able to be solved if a few new converts were to come into the church regularly.

—H. B. L.

# is all the deadwood really dead?

Ron and Marcie knew each other since kindergarten and grew up in a Christ-exalting church. They participated willingly in the classes for children and youth. After high school, they went their separate ways—Ron to the state university and Marcie to work as a flight attendant. In their late 20s, they renewed their friendship, fell in love and decided they couldn't get along without each other. So they married.

By the time of their wedding, faith and the Church had become only optional for them. They were self-sufficient secularists who no longer needed God and had each lived many miles away from their home church for years.

About this time, a new pastor came to that little home church in Vermont. Eager to inspire every member to be the best possible Christian, he began contacting everyone on the membership rolls. He wrote Ron and Marcie to introduce himself and to tell them about new ministries at the church. He urged them to renew their commitment to Christ and to find a church where they would attend faithfully. He enclosed a devotional guide and promised to pray for them every day.

He closed his letter by saying, "Just in case I seem a little bold in writing this letter, let me remind you that you are members of this church. Thus, I bear pastoral responsibility for you. The church cares about you. As your new pastor, I am concerned about your spiritual development. We are contacting every nonactive and nonresident member and urging them to renew the wonderful closeness to Jesus they enjoyed when they joined the church." This thoughtful, loving letter was the first of several that Ron and Marcie received, and it started them back on the road to a quality life with Christ.

Church membership rolls are often treated like mailing lists. It seems important to get rid of dead addresses. Many new pastors are eager to scratch out names and to start with a pure, enthusiastic membership. However, the faith this pastor exhibited reminds us that "old" names are often lonely people who would need renewal and restoration. I want to ask you about your membership roll—is all the deadwood really dead?

As a pastor, I used to feel impatient about names of people on the roll who no longer attended, served or supported the church financially. Of course I am not advocating that you ignore your roll book. Addresses, numbers of children and other information must be kept up-to-date for every member. If someone dies or joins another church, their names must be removed from the list.

But we must thoughtfully consider our redemptive responsibility to the lost, the misplaced, the nonresidents and the backsliders. Though these people seem disinterested, their membership ties to your church may be their only contact with the Kingdom. Such a tenuous contact may not be promising, but it is better than nothing. It may be the bridge they will cross to come home spiritually. You might be surprised to see what happens if you consider these alternatives to dropping the names of inactive people:

*Cherish spiritual history.*

Most churches have requirements for membership. A name doesn't get added to the roll casually; it usually represents someone who once made a deliberate decision to follow Christ. The person behind that name once testified to being born again and pledged to be a part of the visible family of God on earth. Once these men and women cared about eternal issues. Once they wanted to make a difference in the world by serving Christ.

*Try intensifying love.*
Your church may be the only spiritual connection inactive people have with Christ. Try recharging that connection with agape love. Ask your congregation to call these inactive persons' names before God's throne in intercessory prayers. Invite these wayward Christians back—one denomination had a full year's campaign called "Come home where you belong." Express concern about their spiritual condition. Encourage Sunday School classes to reestablish regular contacts. Work to win them as if they were members of your own family.

*Accentuate faithfulness.*
I believe in keeping good records. No church can sustain credibility without integrity at the root of everything it does. But in this matter, we also owe faithfulness to our Savior. I am not suggesting that you deliberately inflate the numbers for your own glory. But do not fall prey to the opposite temptation to whittle the roll down so that the number of members coincides with the average attendance.

Instead of wasting a lot of energy trying to clear the rolls, why not redirect that redemptive energy and emotional fervor to spiritually reactivate the wandering, disappointed, inactive member?

Reaching the lost means winning new people to Christ, but it also involves finding the wandering sheep and binding up the wounds of those who have been hurt. You may have a sibling who is the deadwood on some church list. Think how grateful you would be to a pastor who would love him or her back into Christ's family. Please don't remove names from your membership rolls until you do everything you can to win them back. Your church may represent their only spiritual hope.

—N. B. W.

# more easily preached than lived

Forgiveness stands at the center of the Christian faith. The gospels could easily be subtitled: *God's Instructions for Giving and Receiving Forgiveness.* No one has ever demonstrated forgiveness with greater consistency than our Lord. He expects no less from us.

Forgiveness shows up frequently in Scriptures. God emphasizes forgiveness over and over again in His message to us. If we could only learn to forgive wholeheartedly, as did Christ, we would eliminate many of the frustrating issues of our lives together as human beings. Amazingly, Jesus ties the giving and receiving of forgiveness together—He tells us that no one can receive forgiveness who does not give it.

I remember that once, within a few weeks of each other, two murders were reported on national TV. Two teenage children had been murdered and reporters interviewed the families. As I recall, one set of parents said, "We have forgiven the person who murdered our child. That's what we had to do as Christians, and offering forgiveness gives us inner peace." The other parents said, "We will never forgive the one who killed our son—we can't and we won't." As you might expect, newspapers splashed that headline across their front page: "I will NEVER forgive."

As pastors, we have seen the pain that keeps a family from forgiving. We have also seen the liberty that flows into a family that fully forgives. If forgiveness comes easily, usually the pain has not been great. Yet those who do not forgive add anguish to their inner life. We all know individuals who have suffered years of self-imposed misery because they refused to forgive. Sometimes the people they found difficult to forgive have been dead for years. What torment. What imprisonment. What an agonizing way to live.

I don't know where I heard this story for the first time, but it seems to fit this truth. A famous man died in the prime of life, and newspaper reporters interviewed his mother. "We are writing a story on your son," they said. "We'd like to know at what stage of his life you loved him the most." The reporters persisted with this preposterous question. "Was it when he was a public personality, an author, a celebrity, a teenager or an adult?" After a few moments, the mother replied, "You know, it happened one afternoon when my son was seven. He knew he had hurt me by something he did. As I was reading the paper, my young son rushed into the room. He fell on his knees and buried his face in my lap. As he sobbed, he said, 'Mommy, please forgive me. I'm sorry I hurt you.' He was heartbroken."

The mother continued, "When I think of when I loved him most, it was then."

Somewhat startled by her answer, one of the reporters questioned, "Madam, excuse me, but that seems like such an insignificant happening. Why does that stand out in your mind?"

Her reply is better than a thousand sermons: "I think it was because he needed me to love him so much at that moment."

That is a picture of forgiveness: giving mercy and pardon when people need our love the most. Isn't that exactly what God does? He loves us all the time—but especially when we need it the most.

Forgiveness can be tricky for pastors in relationships with those in the church. Since relationships form the heart of ministry, complications can arise out of those relationships. From our perspective, these troubling people hamper our plans, resist at the wrong time or act immaturely.

Living as we do, in the muddle of human difficulties, it is far easier to preach about forgiveness than to give it. Sadly some pastors carry rancor in their hearts against certain parishioners. One veteran lay leader explained, "Lately, our pastor has been so angry with us that he has been preaching on forgiveness in every service." It is not a pretty sight, nor is it pleasing to the Lord Jesus.

I personally know the pain that failing to forgive brings. One time I flew from Oregon to speak at a conference in Southern California. My mom met me at the airport and asked me immediately, "H. B., are you OK?"

"Yes, Mom, why do you ask?"

"Are you sure you are OK?"

"Yes, yes, Mom; what are you talking about?"

She said, "I thought you might be trying to hide some health problem from me. I heard that your name came up for consideration as pastor of a great church in this area. I also understand the leader said, 'You don't want to consider H. B. because he has had a nervous breakdown.'" And so they didn't.

That report bothered me a lot. Since I was still a young pastor, I was greatly concerned about what others might think about me. I thought this false gossip defamed my reputation. I decided never to speak to that person again. I made a big issue in my mind about this rumor without checking to see if it was true. I am ashamed to admit I carried that nagging pain for years. No one was harmed but me; but I really hurt, even though most of my pain was self-inflicted.

Later, that person became a denominational leader. Then we were forced to work together—perhaps God's way of making me face my attitude. The offender had to communicate with me and

I with him. It was obvious to both of us and to others that a tension existed in the meetings and that between us flowed a negative emotional electricity.

Finally, one day while speaking to this man on the phone, I said quietly, "I have carried this load long enough. I have been indignant since you misrepresented me years ago at such and such a church. No promotion or important pastorate could wipe away the pain I felt toward you since you wronged me."

Then I continued, calling him by name, "From this day forward, as far as I am concerned, the incident never happened. I forgive you. I ask you to forgive me for allowing something I didn't even know to be true to color my thinking about you. Please forgive me."

He was shocked, and so was I. The words seemed to tumble out of my mouth; I really didn't intend to speak so frankly. His response was what it nearly always is—a positive one. As a result, both of us experienced a feeling of release and relief. Now we could work together with no feeling of alienation. We were free of what had us bound.

But let's admit it, forgiveness is hard to do sometimes. We need God to soften our hearts and to make us ready to forgive. Forgiveness does not always come easily to the natural human heart, especially if we have been wronged and wounded. Ephesians 4:32 is the pattern: "Be . . . compassionate to one another, forgiving each other, just as in Christ God has forgave you." The compassionate Christ makes available an amazing empowerment that transforms relationships—even the most troubled ones.

Sometimes a pastor needs to seek forgiveness of individuals in the congregation—listen to what the Lord tells you in your quiet times about your attitudes toward people. Sometimes, a pastor needs to stand before the congregation and say, "I am sorry. I did something wrong. I misled you. I spoke before I thought. You should be able to count on me to be like Christ; I am sorry."

Don't think you will lose the respect, if you admit mistakes. Most members of your congregation will honor you when they see you acting in conformity to the principles you preach. The majority will respect your transparency and vulnerability. They will be glad to know you are open to the Lord's direction. Such a confessional approach to ministry will help create an accepting climate in your church. I believe that is how God wants His churches to be. Many pastors could revolutionize their ministry immediately if they could bring themselves to say sincerely:

"I want to apologize for the feelings I've had."

"I was wrong."

"I want to ask for forgiveness for attitudes I showed in last Sunday's sermon."

"I want to admit how destructive my self-pity has become."

Let's consider practical, true-to-Scripture ways to make our ministry models of Christian forgiveness:

*Apply preaching to self.*
Refuse to preach on forgiveness until you are sure there is no lack of forgiveness in your heart toward anyone. Authentic preaching requires us to be living examples of what we preach. Preaching about forgiveness will be a counterfeit exercise if you know you have not forgiven others.

*Practice forgiveness without limits.*
The apostle Peter thought it would be generous and merciful to forgive another person seven times. Jesus corrected Peter by saying "seventy-seven times" (Matt.

18:22). Apparently that means no score keeping.

### Check the forgiveness issue when praying seems difficult.

No one can be confused after reading this clear-as-day Scripture: "If you are offering your gift at the altar and there remember that your brother has something against you, leave your gift there in front of the altar. First go and be reconciled to your brother; then come and offer your gift" (Matt. 5:23,24). If I read the passage correctly, we are to seek out the one who has something against us, rather than wait for them to come to us.

### Seeking forgiveness shapes future conduct.

When I ask someone to forgive me, it imprints something in me that keeps me from committing that offense again. Asking others for forgiveness may be painful, but it helps us grow in Christlikeness. I think God created the process to make our conduct and attitudes more like His.

### Live by Paul's liberating advice.

"Be even-tempered, content with second place, quick to forgive an offense. Forgive as quickly and completely as the Master forgives you. And regardless of what else you put on, wear love. It's your basic, all-purpose garment. Never be without it." (Col. 3:13,14, *THE MESSAGE*). What a passage. And what a free life the passage promises.

—H. B. L.

# the amazing power of peacemaking

One of saddest experiences I can remember was the time I had a misunderstanding with a couple in my church. This miscommunication was never resolved. We parted on friendly terms, but not as friends. To bring closure to the relationship, I invited them to join me at a meeting with a staff member they admired. I allowed them to express their opinion about me and my ministry. The pain was excruciating—far worse than I had imagined—but it finally ended. The couple made their point, and I listened. We shook hands, and they walked out of my life. I still wish it could have ended differently. I have agonized for years about the failure of that relationship.

Conflict management is a hot topic these days. Many clever books and seminars are available on the subject. The presupposition is that a pastor should know how to keep parishioners from harming each other emotionally or spiritually. Some approaches also imply that a minister well trained in conflict management will be able to predict or even produce a certain desired outcome.

But why is conflict management needed? One theory holds that conflict is inevitable because it is brought about by change. The theory seems reasonable, until you check the Bible to see what it says about peace.

Recently, I overheard a group of Christians talking about a church official who leads conflict management seminars. They remarked as they laughed, "Without the leader's dictatorial ways, there would be no conflict to manage." I don't laugh when I hear such a commentary. I am saddened to think that Christian leaders might cause conflict in the churches they have been called to serve. I long to follow Christ and to have the courage, if necessary, to lay down my life for His sheep. The least we can do as pastors is to bring the salve of tenderness to the wounded sheep.

Jesus often taught about peacemaking. He gave such a high priority to peace in His earthly ministry, that we must strive for it in the Church. His words call me to be like Him and to pursue peace: "Blessed are the peacemakers, for they will be called sons of God" (Matt. 5:9). In whatever translation you read this verse, it comes out about the same—those who make peace enjoy a special relationship to God.

My soul was recently nourished again by the record of Jesus' words as He prepared to leave His disciples: "I've told you all this so that trusting me, you will be unshakable and assured, deeply at peace. In this godless world you will continue to experience difficulties. But take heart! I've conquered the world" (John 16:33, *THE MESSAGE*). "You will be . . . deeply at peace"—what a reassuring promise.

Paul's instruction to the Colossian church about peace sounds like problem-solving guidance for contemporary church decision-making groups: "Let the peace of Christ keep you in tune with each other, in step with each other. None of this going off and doing your own thing" (Col. 3:15, *THE MESSAGE*). I love those lofty words-"Let the peace of Christ keep you in tune with each other."

Years ago I checked a book by William Barclay, the English New Testament scholar, to be sure I understood what this passage means. I discovered three things. One, "peace," in this context, is translated from *shalom*, which is not merely an absence of trouble between individuals but is a peace that wishes the highest possible good for the other person. Two, the blessing promised by Jesus is given to the peacemaker, the one who works actively to bring about peace. And three, peacemaking is the work God wants us to do in the world, in relationships and in the Church. What a lifelong challenge this passage presents to pastors.

Making peace is a thousand times more satisfying than managing conflict. True peacemakers pursue peace by the way they live, by the way they react to people and by the way they accept people they meet along the journey of ministry.

Let me be candid. Some pastors continually create conflict. Though they blame others, they are the cause. I know a passive/aggressive pastor who causes lots of conflict and then holds the coats of those he incited. Some combative pastors have their emotional fists ready at the least provocation. I know that occasionally in a ministry it is necessary to wage a stouthearted, all-out scrimmage for righteousness. But I beg you to be absolutely certain that the offense is against the gospel and that it is not something you have caused. Why not search your heart now; is there someone you should call or write to make peace?

Pastors experience great inner turmoil when those with whom they are in conflict need a pastor. What will such a minister do when the parishioner receives bad news at the hospital or when their teenage kid runs away? Think what it is like to lead a funeral for someone with whom you had an ugly conflict or antagonism. As the years go by, these incidents from the past undermine your personal peace with God.

The peacemaking that God wants for us also applies to other ministers. A hint of gossip seems so innocent until the accumulation is considered. Dream a holy dream with me: What would happen in each church throughout the world if every minister committed to being a peacemaker?

The peacemaking pastor possesses a quiet strength that points congregants to the Lord. They admire one who brings peace into every situation. That kind of minister can unite a divided church in a few months by bringing each member into contact with the Prince of Peace.

My prayer for every pastor reading these pages is that you may be fulfilled as you commit yourself to becoming the peacemaker God wants you to become. Let's think about ways to help answer that prayer:

*Examine your own part in peacemaking.*
Try testing yourself by Thomas à Kempis's self-judging words: "All men desire peace, but few desire the things that make for peace."[1]

*Put others in the best light.*
If others seem abrasive, simply overlook the problem and conclude they are having a bad day. Or perhaps you have misread a situation. Give them the benefit of the doubt just as you wanted others to do the last time you had a bad day.

*Refuse to take part in an "ain't it awful" discussion.*
Sometimes your staunch supporters come to you after someone has criticized you and say, "Isn't it awful what they said?" Please don't enter into such a trap. It will wither your spirit and make you feel small. This same person may use the "Ain't it awful" technique *against* you tomorrow. As a leader, learn to absorb the hit caused by a controversial decision in the church. Resist self-pity—it is destructive.

*Speak often about Jesus, the peacemaker.*

Preach about Him. Talk about Him in small groups. Promote peace wherever you go. Conflicts, suspicions, antagonisms and hostilities are always harmful. Often, troubled people mirror the attitudes of the environment of the church they attend. Thus, an improvement in your attitude sometimes starts improving the whole situation. Lead your congregation to live satisfying lives by following Paul's directive: "Live in harmony and peace. And may the God of love and peace be with you" (2 Cor. 13:11, *TLB*).

*Look for ways to make peace.*

Whenever there is a misunderstanding, don't move in right away to be the prophet or to set things right. Take the time to seek the mind of Christ to know how you can make peace; then you will come back to the situation with a clearer perspective, a quieter spirit or a softly spoken word. Remember that a kind deed always wins, even when the conflict seems the hottest.

—H. B. L.

**Note**

1. Rebecca Davis and Susan Mesner, eds., *The Treasury of Religious and Spiritual Quotations* (Pleasantville, NY: Reader's Digest Association, 1994), p. 385.

# admit it— change is scary!

I remember the experience well, like it were yesterday. As pastor of my sweetheart church at Pompano Beach, Florida, I was hosting our guest speaker. He was a veteran churchman, well known and loved by thousands. I was eager to understand his heartbeat for evangelism and to learn from his years of experience. We were driving south on Federal Highway, a few blocks from the famous Coral Ridge Presbyterian Church. I was enjoying our informative discussions about ministry.

At a quiet lapse in our conversation, my friend remarked without any apparent context or connection, "You know, he's an apostle of change without purpose."

"Who are we talking about?" I asked.

He replied, "You know, we're talking about Pastor Williams, out in the West."

I was nonplussed for a moment. How did such a comment relate to our conversation? I expected some explanation—and I didn't have long to wait.

Like an old sage, the veteran leader, with his quick mind and long experience, observed, "Pastor Williams is an apostle of change for no reason. That's why he's in hot water most of the time."

For days afterward I wondered if my trusted friend was speaking in generalities or if he wanted me to slow down change in the church I served. A decade later I still think often about his remark. His observation forced me to remember a bedrock principle—do not make change unless it accomplishes something significant.

Let's think carefully about change in our churches. Is it a nuisance, or does it represent new possibilities? And how can the pastor know the difference between necessary change, which will enable the gospel of Christ to do its work in the hearts of your people, and futile change created to please someone's whims? Do we know the difference? If we believe change is necessary, how can we bring people to embrace it wholeheartedly?

*Progress requires change.*

Think about every advance you have ever experienced. Almost immediately, it becomes apparent that every small step of progress required someone to change, and perhaps change a lot. If progress equals change, then change equals potential conflict. Perhaps we need to be more sensitive to those who resist change. When they oppose change, it may not be because they are cranky, disloyal, selfish or stingy. They may simply be terrorized. Change is not always progress, but no progress is possible without change.

*Timing matters.*

Some changes can only occur within a narrow window of opportunity. Before is too soon and after is too late. Flowers never grow in winter, and snow never falls in summer. There are seasons to plant, cultivate and harvest concepts, ministries and programs. A proposal that was rejected five years ago may work well today. Don't fall for the idea-killing sentence "We tried that before and it didn't work." Sometimes conditions, attitudes or even personnel have changed since the idea was previously suggested. If the door is open, walk through it. If it is shut, it might not be a good idea to kick it in.

*Reasons for change must be carefully communicated ahead of time.* With little forethought and no explanation, a pastor I know removed the pulpit, publicly ridiculed hymnals, replaced the organ with a guitar and received the offering at the door as people left. When he met tough resistance, he felt discouraged and wounded. Is it any wonder? He neither understood nor explained his changes. In fact, he told a lay leader that "every church needs to be shaken up occasionally." He unnecessarily unnerved his congregation, and they forced his resignation.

*Try refurbishing existing ministries.*
Before attempting radical surgery, try infusing new meaning and creative energy into existing ministries to make them more effective. Variety, resourcefulness and originality are often accepted enthusiastically when applied to existing ministries. I recently stayed in a lovely refurbished old inn on the New Jersey seashore. It was considerably more efficient and comfortable and by far more aesthetically pleasing than any new hotel by the freeway. Try refurbishing worship, Sunday School and your midweek prayer meeting. Most congregations can accept innovations in small increments, whereas catastrophic change may push someone over the edge. Try changing one thing at a time, instead of doing it all at once.

*Everyone sometimes resists change.*
Conflict arises not only when pastors change things. We pastors can be just as resistant to the changes sug-

gested by our members. A forward-looking woman in her 80s was overheard to say at a seminar on change, "Our pastor loves change, just as long as he thinks it up."

*Methods matter.*
It is logical and even necessary that ministry methods should change from year to year and from generation to generation. But be warned: Churches divide more often over methods than over doctrine. Since there are many ways to accomplish most goals, a leader should be flexible regarding methodology while keeping absolutely resolute concerning mission and message. Whatever the method, every component or phase of ministry must be done in ways that honor Christ and enrich people.

*Essence must be retained.*
Since saving the lost and making disciples of them are equal parts of Christ's Great Commission, these two tasks must be preserved and regularly refreshed. The New Testament requires worship, preaching, intercessory prayer and fellowship. These components of a church's ministry must be taken seriously and continually renewed.

As the times change, the Church must change strategies to communicate the unchanging good news about Christ. Though she probably did not have the Church in mind, Catherine the Great (A.D. 1729-96) understood our dilemma about change when she said, "A great wind [of change] is blowing, and that either gives you imagination or a headache."[1] It is so easy to walk right past great opportunities because they would require someone to change, maybe us.

—N. B. W.

**Note**

1. Louis E. Boone, *Quotable Business* (New York: Random House, 1992), p. 301.

# caring referrals to christian counselors

The need for authentic Christian counseling keeps increasing in our confused culture.

Several facts have created this buildup. Critical personal issues and family breakdown are mushrooming. Problems seem more traumatic and frequent. More committed Christian counselors are available with more specialized training than pastors receive in seminary. At the same time, more and more believers seem willing to discuss their inner pain and work through tough issues. And more dysfunctional persons seek the stability Christ and His Church provide. How grateful we must be for the counselor-helpers God has given us.

If all these issues were added to a pastor's duties, it becomes obvious that no minister could make it. In response and as a remedy to all this brokenness, God has given the Christian community many gifted counselors to augment and strengthen the day-to-day efforts of contemporary ministers.

Once the pastor recognizes these increasing needs, identifying competent counselors is the natural step. The minister must feel comfortable trusting congregants to the care of such specialists. What pastors are not able to do for members and attendees because of time and training limitations can be provided by competent counselors.

Several years ago, the American Association of Christian Counselors asked me to list the characteristics Christian counselors needed to exhibit before I would recommend them to my people. Here is what I suggested as being absolutely essential:

*Exude trust and confidentiality.*
Everyone has a right to expect confidentiality from a counselor. No discussion with others about the individual's problems is ever allowed.

*Be a good listener.*
People need a counselor to truly hear them. Although some pastors are good listeners, they are trained to talk more than to listen. Their preaching and teaching skills are the main focus of their ministry most of the week. Thus, it is often disconcerting for a pastor to sit for long periods of time listening. But a counselor must listen well.

*Act emotionally mature.*
Ineffective counselors may use our parishioners as personal confidants, revealing his or her own weakness to the person seeking help. It becomes like the blind leading the blind. This type of counselor is dangerous and should be avoided.

*Exhibit integrity.*
The desire to be a counselor is not sufficient to make someone a good counselor. Integrity in all aspects of counseling must be displayed. A trial period can be useful if a pastor is willing to monitor the progress of those who use a particular counselor. Here are some areas to examine in determining the quality of a counseling program:

• Training

Where was this counselor trained? What level of education does the person have? What do we know about his or her experience? How does faith inform treatment strategies? A counselor with no commitment to Christ often does a believer more harm than good.

• Affordability

A counselors should not be expected to work without compensation. In fact, some authorities believe that emotionally needy persons make better progress with a counselor who charges them fees than they do with a pastor, whom the parishioners expect to help them without pay. Three questions must be answered in determining the cost of counseling: (1) How many sessions are required? (2) What is the hourly fee? and (3) Can a client use an insurance plan?

• Theology

I can only enthusiastically recommend a counselor who is on the same track as I am theologically. If the counselee is a member of my congregation, the counselor must not confuse the person seeking help about how we relate our lives to God, prayer, the Bible and living the holy life.

• Diligence

Counselors needs a specific treatment plan for every person he or she sees. The goal of counseling needs to be evaluated periodically. Good records must be maintained. Progress should be noted from session to session.

• Team player

The healing community needs its players to work together. So those seeking help should know that the pastor, physician, psychiatrist and Christian counselor are working together as a team to help them get well. Usually the Christian counselor must see to it that everyone is working in unity.

*Communicate.*

Good communication among the counselor, the counselee and the pastor is crucial. The counselor must also be available to the needy person by phone so that a call for help in an emergency is always answered.

As a pastor, I usually saw troubled individuals only once or twice before suggesting a counselor. During these meetings I worked hard to communicate my concern. We had what I call a Christian conversation to assess whether their issues were spiritual or emotional. If I felt they needed more help, I would take time in these sessions to tell them why I thought they should be referred to another person. I explained that they would have more time with a professional counselor—someone who was technically trained to help them solve a particular issue.

Many pastors see troubled people too many times before referring them to a Christian counselor. A counselors usually has more training and more experience in dealing with specific problems. My other duties did not leave me time enough to delve deeply into their problems. I always thought of a referral to a counselor in the same way as a referral to a physician. I would sometimes joke, "I don't know how to fix broken legs, and I can't fix messed-up childhoods."

One other reason kept me from listening to too much of their story. I found that if people told me too much, they would often quit attending church because they were embarrassed that their minister knew so much about them.

The secret of good referrals, however, is to know a counselor so well that you have absolute confidence in the good that your church member will receive. Counseling must help, not hinder, Christian growth in your church members. How does a pastor develop such a relationship with a Christian counselor?

*Make the first move.*
Inquire among other ministers in your community as to the competence and faith commitment of counselors in your area. When a name surfaces several times from these conversations, call that counselor and set up a conference or lunch to get acquainted. At that meeting, ask about issues that matter most to you.

*Consider providing office space.*
Some churches offer office space to a counselor in exchange for lower fees to the congregation. Some churches even consider this person to be a staff member of the local congregation, so the counselor is asked to attend staff meetings and is sometimes given platform privileges so members of the church will identify with him or her.

*Encourage beginning counselors.*
Providing office space and free access to your congregation may be the enticement needed to encourage a

beginning counselor to move to your community. You can work out arrangements for shared facilities like those I suggested above.

*Create a climate of acceptance of counseling.*
Help your people understand that Christian counseling may help them with problems that have bothered them for years. Refuse to joke about mental illness.

*Get victory over needing to know everything.*
Some pastors feel threatened by the fact that a counselor may know more about a parishioner than they do. Get over it. You can pastor a person just as well if you don't know all the pain from their past. Even though they have a counselor, they will still tell you plenty. The counselor should become for you a friend, a burden bearer and a Christian colleague.

—H. B. L.

# the Leader

who trusts

through

triumph and

tragedy

# lessons learned through tragedies and trials

Tragedies and unexpected difficulties often occur at times and in manners we cannot explain. That's the way it was after I invited Ridge Ireland and his wife to interview for a staff position in our church. The interview went especially well, and we invited them to join our team. They accepted the assignment with enthusiasm, and we were excited about their coming.

They went home to California to prepare and pack for the move. The long-awaited day finally arrived. Ridge would drive a U-Haul truck containing all their belongings, and his wife would drive their car, with their small child and a babysitter who was coming along to help.

For some undetermined reason—no one knows why to this day—a terrible one-car accident occurred. The wife lost control of the automobile and all three—wife, baby and babysitter—were killed instantly.

For Ridge, this became the worst trial of his life. This inexplicable and seemingly useless tragedy was soon the ultimate test of his faith. Where could he find support? Where should he go—back to California, or on to Salem? What did life and ministry hold for him now? Why? Why? Why? There was no answer. In his anguished cry of why, I heard the echoes of our Savior. "God, God, why have you abandoned me?" It is a great comfort that Jesus Himself cried out "Why?" even though He knew God's will was good.

When Ridge lost his family, our church struggled to know what to do. But I listened to my heart and flew to the area where the accident occurred. I arrived to walk beside this young husband and father, whose life had crumbled under him. He was shocked, broken and perplexed. Though our professional relationship was only starting, the most pressing immediate task was to be a pastor to him—to show Ridge God's love.

The congregation faced the challenge of reaching across the miles, binding the wounds of this hurting new friend, and trying not to argue with God about this terrible loss. Everyone was eager to help, but how? I am proud that our church lived out its beliefs about compassion.

In fact, in this situation, their care of Ridge reminded me of the words of Jesus: "Here is a simple, rule-of-thumb guide for behavior: Ask yourself what you want people to do for you, then grab the initiative and do it for them" (Matt. 7:12, *THE MESSAGE*).

Good and bad news came from these tragic circumstances. The bad news was that a young minister lost his family and because of the move had no in-place support system to help him through his grief. The good news was that when he came to our congregation, he was loved, cared for, and treated with admiration. They took Ridge in as one of Christ's needy children, which he was. Our church welcomed him as a staff member and found joy in becoming the family of God to him.

After a year or two of healing, Ridge married a young lady in our church and now they have two children. I believe Ridge is a living example of Paul's great words of encouragement: "We continue to shout our praise even when we're hemmed in with troubles, because we know how troubles can develop passionate patience in us, and how that patience in turn forges the tempered steel of virtue, keeping us alert for whatever God will do next" (Rom. 5:3,4, *THE MESSAGE*).

Ridge has now served the Lord diligently and effectively as a staff pastor for 30 years. Those who know his story, stand in awe of his inspiring example of God's grace and staying power in the most agonizing of tragedies. He doesn't talk much about his previous pain. It's almost as though he were an onlooker at a very sad occurrence. But when you know him and see his steadfast service to the Lord, you realize that his life and ministry were strengthened by his tenacity and childlike dependence on God. That faith simply said, "I don't understand these events. But I'm not going to allow despair to destroy my life and ministry."

As a pastor, I saw many hard-to-explain trials come to people under my care. I'm sure that you, too, have experienced the unexplainable. The thing I have noticed over and over is that those who have a viable faith and realize how much God loves them are able to make it through the tough times and go on to a life of victory. Their lives are filled with great commitment in the face of tragedy and pain. However, those who blame God and roll up into a ball of self-pity find their lives blighted and scarred forever.

I am convinced that going on with the Lord is a thousand times better than stopping to look for answers to the unanswerable. As it has been said, we either become better or bitter as we face tragedies and trials.

God expects us, as pastors, to be specialists in helping His children find faith even in their darkest midnights. It is our God-enabled directive to help hurting folks heal. Though it causes us pain as well, the task of standing with God's people as they suffer is one of our greatest privileges. They will lean on our faith and hear us say by our lives and our lips, "God loves you and wants to help you through this difficulty." In being there for them, we represent Christ, who promises His faithful presence to His children when they are in distress.

Find a way to use every test and trial as a bridge of ministry to the hurting. You don't need to try to explain suffering or pain. Just be there, as a friend, a member of the family, a representative of Christ. Here are several suggestions for offering God's strength in the moments of great grief and suffering:

*Follow your heart when a tragedy strikes.*
Drop everything else and go represent Jesus to those suffering loss or experiencing hurt. Even if it is your day off or you are not dressed in clerical clothes, go help needy people lean on the strong arm of the Savior. They will never forget your ministry to them in their pain.

*Specialize in the ministry of presence.*
Hurting folks want you with them in the tough times because you represent Christ. They believe all will be well when you offer them ministry in the name of our Lord. It is not the messenger who is special, but the One whom the messenger represents.

*Depend on the church members.*
A river of redemptive compassion flows from the hearts of the family of God. Encourage your congregation to provide Christlike acts of kindness and support. Their faithfulness and love will amaze and bless you. And by exercising these holy qualities, the lives of those who receive and those who give are always enriched.

*Get ready for tragedies.*
All of us have problems at some time in our lives. Veteran clergy will tell you that some of their most productive ministries took place when they were going

through their own valleys and the Christians in their congregation saw that their leader's faith worked in suffering, as well as in the good times.

I love the witness of an old saint who said, "Years ago I saw a pastor go through the valley of the shadow of death. Up until then I always thought of Christianity as a nice idea and a good ideal. But when I saw the strength of that minister's faith, I concluded I needed what he had. When I asked him about it, he said, 'Let me show you to Jesus.' And I said, 'You already have.' "

—H. B. L.

# transforming obstacles into opportunities

I once led a series of pastors' conferences on eight college campuses. On the walls and bulletin boards, mood posters were hung everywhere. One of them read, "When given a lemon, make lemonade."

An influential speaker won the crowd when he remarked, "Why did someone put that poster near the front of the auditorium when I was about to speak?" Everyone laughed—though not a knock-em-dead, deep belly laugh. The chuckles seemed to say, "I've been there."

It's true—every ministry has more than its share of hindrances. One of the most difficult things for a pastor to accept is to be stopped by obstacles. Sometimes we accept hindrances that need to be challenged and changed.

Remember, it is one of Christianity's hallmarks that for 2,000 years it has miraculously transformed obstacles into opportunities. The record is amazing—what seemed impossible has been accomplished. Little has become much. Small has grown to big. Tough has become tender. Across two millennia, God's power working through human beings has transformed apparent impossibilities into glorious victories.

The Old and New Testaments, the history books and the many testimonies of modern Christians all remind us to celebrate God's faithfulness. God threw the Egyptian army into the sea, used hail and locusts, storms and drought to accomplish His will. He sent fire from heaven and blinded the eyes of His enemies. He gave children to those in old age and delivered His people using the weakest human servants. In the New Testament, He defeated the devil in the wilderness, raised the dead and gave vision back to the blind. He turned a motley crew of fishermen into a group of leaders who turned the world upside down. Most of all, He snapped the iron grip of death, throwing off its tyranny and bursting from the grave. He poured out His Spirit on young and old, men and women, and empowered them to speak the good news of His love to the ends of the earth. Since the day of Christ's ascension to heaven, He has, by His Spirit, enabled His Church to withstand the onslaught of persecutions and division, heresies and harassment so that His command could be fulfilled, to tell all men of the great and glorious gospel of Jesus. His name is Emmanuel, God with us.

Even today, God's mighty hand is working. Every established ministry of every contemporary church has at one time faced seemingly insurmountable difficulties. Turning obstacles into opportunities, with God's help, is something Christians do well. God's miracles shine out in the dark of despair and doubt.

The notion of useful obstacles does not sound inspiring. But trials, by exercising our faith and our souls, build patience and endurance. When persistence results, then Kingdom efforts finally succeed beyond our wildest dreams. Difficulties disappear, hardships become blessings, and battles bring victory. Take courage from several examples from Scripture.

The boy Jesus, at 12 years of age, turned His trip to the temple from a family crisis into a time when learned religious leaders were amazed at "his understanding and his answers" (Luke 2:47). Who would have believed the old guys would listen to the young guy? But they did.

Consider the time Jesus healed a man beside the pool, who had been an invalid for 38 years. Those long years of suffering were the foundation on which our Lord built the testimony of His power. The man's suffering was transformed into an undeniable witness to the power of Christ, which silenced the Jewish skeptics (see John 5:1-15). The cripple's longtime difficulty was transformed into a long-remembered opportunity for the gospel.

In the ministry of the disciples we continue to see God transforming obstacles into opportunities. When Peter and John healed a crippled beggar at the temple gate, we see God using the incident in the history of His Church, turning an obstacle into an opportunity. The healing created a chaotic debate in the Sanhedrin (see Acts 3,4).

Paul transformed appalling obstacles into exciting opportunities when he sang praise choruses at midnight in jail. God sent an earthquake that shook open the prison and the jailer believed—that's obstacle-defying and opportunity-inspiring singing at its best.

Take courage from Joshua. When he urged God's people forward, he faced insurmountable odds. But the greater the difficulty, the wider and broader and stronger are God's promises of aid and deliverance. God's extravagant promise to Joshua says, "I will give you every place where you set your foot. . . . Your territory will extend from the desert to Lebanon, and from the great river, the Euphrates—all the Hittite country—to the Great Sea on the west. No one will be able to stand up against you all the days of your life. . . . I will never leave you nor forsake you" (Josh. 1:3-5). Who could ask for anything more? The hindrances seem small when compared to the promise.

One could easily dwell on the litany of hindrances in Joshua's situation: timidity, fear, disobedience and discouragement. Although the passage is candid about the obstacles, it shows us the rich future God has planned for them and for us. As the apostle Paul put it, "For our light and momentary troubles are achieving for us an eternal glory that far outweighs them all. So we fix our eyes not on what is seen, but on what is unseen" (2 Cor. 4:17,18).

All of this started my musing about how we might turn obstacles into opportunities. How can we transform setbacks into comebacks? Here's my short list:

*Transform apathy into achievement.*
Sometimes pastors expect people to invest more energy in Christian service than their spiritual life generates. Apathy is often a symptom of anemic faith. Unfortunately, a church too often acts like a restaurant that asks people to contribute financially to keep the business open, rather than serve them top-quality food. Good food builds successful restaurants and healthy customers. In a similar way, spiritual nourishment builds effective churches and mature Christians. Apathy may also be rooted in boredom. If people are asked to commit to a cause that is too small, or to give out more than they are able, they will become bored or overextended. For a church to be boring contradicts the gospel. But it happens. A pastor may call people to help paint the church, cut the lawn or give another $20. Of course, there is nothing wrong with such service to the church. But people want to do ministry that makes a difference for someone or helps another to find eternal life. On the other hand, those who feel apathetic because they are overextended need a loving pastor to help them unpack their lives so they have time to find

satisfaction in service to Christ through His Church.

*Transform hunger into spirituality.*
A hollow emptiness exists in every human heart. In our society, gloomy cynicism has replaced liberating optimism. We have lost confidence in our government, our schools and our churches.

But in the midst of pessimism, we are still searching for something good and right, something to sustain us spiritually and to help us make sense of life. Books like William Bennett's *The Book of Virtues* become best-sellers, and books about spiritual formation have gained widespread popularity even in secular bookstores. We pastors know that a counterfeit spirituality will never fill the void that the love of God the Redeemer alone can satisfy. But I believe that the twenty-first century will be an unprecedented moment in human history for Christians to live out.

*Transform division into reconciliation.*
I use "reconciliation" as an eight-cylinder word to describe the unifying energy of Christ in human relationships. These relationships include marriages, families, churches, committees, schools, communities, work places, countries, cultures and any other situation where alienation reigns.

As we all know, authentic reconciliation is not possible without the enablement of the Spirit of God. But His reconciling power is enough to heal old feuds, to eliminate competition between believers and to quell struggles for control. And with reconciliation much of the spiritual short-circuiting in many churches disappears.

*Transform fuzziness into clarity.*

Fuzzy Bible teaching keeps sinners from salvation and hinders believers from spiritual growth. Current problems of doctrinal and moral confusion can only be solved with crystal-clear biblical preaching and teaching that can be easily understood by common folks. Although a minister of the gospel should never be personally offensive, we must not give in to the temptation to keep quiet about Christ's challenge. No matter how unpopular we may become, we are conscience bound to proclaim Christ and His gospel. Many factors militate against clarity and forthrightness these days, but the spiritual survival of converts and the stability of believers depend on it.

So much for my list of obstacles and opportunities. They are probably different from yours. But whether your list is like mine or not, why not take your most frustrating obstacles to God in earnest, straightforward prayer. Ask Him to turn them into your greatest blessings for the sake of His kingdom. The great head of the Church wants to transform your obstacles into opportunities and your hindrances into victories.

—N. B. W.

# character really matters

Does character count for pastors? According to a *Newsweek* magazine, it really matters:

> Charismatic clergy have the added aura of representing God or channeling the Holy Spirit. That's why Billy Graham, for example, decided early in his ministry never to be alone with a woman other than his wife. Few others are so fastidious. A generation ago, philandering clergy usually lost their jobs. That still happens. But in our age when adultery is tolerated in political and other leaders, religious denominations are hesitant to set too high a standard for their own. What some Protestant denominations seem to believe is that sexual behavior is either too personal to legislate or too trivial to condemn.[1]

In today's permissive moral environment, it sometimes seems easy to accept the prevailing opinion that character doesn't matter all that much. But I have seen men's lives destroyed when they give in to such thinking and allow themselves to walk down the path of sexual immorality or other grievous sins.

"H. B., I have destroyed my ministry and family with a stupid sexual sin." A one-sentence confession like that has become too common. You hear it secondhand about fellow students you knew in college or seminary. You hear it from lay leaders about former ministers. You hear pastors discuss how easily they could have been drawn into such a heartbreaking situation. Notice the accuracy of that one-sentence confession that sexual sin and stupidity stand side by side. After the attraction dims and the adventure is past and the wreckage begins, sexual sin shows itself to be downright stupid.

Pastors who compromise moral purity quickly come to understand how much their behavior displeases God. Though at first they may be tempted to justify themselves, they soon learn from sad experience just how much irreparable damage such sin provokes. It destroys their peace of mind and their quality of life. It often causes them to lose their family, their ministry, their good standing in the community, their Christian friendships and their self-respect. That's a lot to give up for the short-lived excitement of a fling. A morally ruined preacher is a sad picture because credibility is forever compromised and the future is most often bleak.

Listen to Paul's timeless challenge: "Among you there must not be even a hint of sexual immorality" (Eph. 5:3). What a sobering admonition to us in a time of such moral casualness—"not be even a hint." In the same chapter, Paul indicates the way to live in victory in these matters: "Be imitators of God" (Eph. 5:1). Every reader in Ephesus understood his meaning. Paul adds, "Nor should there be obscenity, foolish talk or coarse joking, which are out of place, but rather thanksgiving" (Eph. 5:4).

In my office mail nearly every day comes an alarming assortment of anecdotes, articles and information from pastors and other Christians, proving how overwhelmingly present is a declining morality, due to sexual sins, pornography, off-color humor and Internet rubbish. Whenever a highly visible minister falls into disrepute, all ministers are weakened. Indeed, the name of our dear Savior is dragged in the mud.

Pastors are particularly at risk for sexual sin. They have few close friends, are the target of scheming members of the opposite sex and experience a high level of stress in their marriages and families and to whom they have to answer. Any one of these pressures might tempt a pastor to cut moral corners in speech or relationships. But it *does not have to happen* to you. The Bible tells us to resist temptation and it will flee from us—and it will.

In speaking at pastors' conferences, I encourage pastors to resist sexual temptations by using a guideline created by pastor Rick Warren of Saddleback Valley Community Church in California:

1. Thou shalt not visit the opposite sex alone at their home.
2. Thou shalt not counsel the opposite sex alone in your office.
3. Thou shalt not counsel the opposite sex more than once without that person's mate being present.
4. Thou shalt not go to lunch or be alone in public with a member of the opposite sex.
5. Thou shalt not kiss any attender of the opposite sex or show affection that could be questioned.
6. Thou shalt not discuss detailed sexual problems with members of the opposite sex in counseling.
7. Thou shalt not discuss thy marriage problems with members of the opposite sex.
8. Thou shalt be careful in answering cards and letters from members of the opposite sex.
9. Thou shalt make thy secretary and thy wife thy protective allies in counseling.

10. Thou shalt pray for the integrity of staff members and colleagues in ministry.[2]

Problems of credibility arise not only from actual events but also from questionable appearance in behavior and relationships. Careless conduct bites like a mad dog even when there is no actual sin.

I hear some readers saying, "H. B., I serve in a small church and the people expect me to visit them." Of course you must continue to visit your members, but use common sense and street smarts. Make sure there is more than one person at home. Stand at the door unless you are sure someone else is there. Take someone with you when you call. In every possible way, build a high hedge of protection around your marriage, so all know that you are committed for life to your spouse.

In our writings and along the pastoral conference trail, Neil and I have offered tried-and-true advice for building a high hedge around your marriage. Here's a short list of what we believe to be satisfying ways to create a happy clergy marriage and to build a hedge that protects the minister of God from many temptations to sexual sin:

- Live by the highest possible code of conduct.
- Find a prayer partner.
- Keep the home fires burning.
- Learn from others' failures.
- Maintain your resistance.
- Remember real pastors control their appetites.
- Maintain balance in your life.
- Establish accountability.
- Nurture soul friends.

- Seek marriage counseling quickly when you sense a problem.

Though it is seldom discussed, a high percentage of sexual sins committed by pastors starts with inappropriate counseling practices. Shoddy relationships are allowed to develop. However, many of these problems can be avoided before they start. Here's how. Carefully think through your counseling atmosphere. How is the furniture arranged? What mood is set by the layout of the room? Is there some kind of physical barrier, such as a desk between you and your counselee? What subtle messages do you send in your counseling sessions? How can you maintain an accepting atmosphere mood without falling into compromising overtones?

Is your office isolated? Do you keep the door open when you are alone with someone? Do you keep plenty of lovely pictures of your spouse and children on the desk? Do you mention your wife or husband with appreciation and affection? Use any sensible means you can think of to exude the message, "I love my wife. I'm not fair game."

Now let me list specific ways to help you pass the moral credibility test with flying colors:

*Apply Paul's teachings.*
Steep yourself in the perspective that Paul outlines in Ephesians 5:1-21. Paul gives wonderful recommendations shaped by the reasoned way he lived his own life and did his ministry.

*Strengthen your marriage.*
Right now, I beg you to stop reading and make a list of practical ways to improve your marriage. Mail a card,

send flowers, buy a negligee, arrange a short trip out of town, offer to help with more household tasks, take your spouse out to dinner or plan a family outing that is not interrupted by any church obligation. Most ministry couples will do their marriage a fulfilling favor by giving more attention to issues of communication, affection, intimacy and sexual fulfillment. With a little extra enjoyable effort, you can be so much more for each other than anybody outside your marriage could ever be.

*Speak often of your admiration for your spouse.*
Church members will appreciate this part of the hedge you are building. They will admire this quality and perhaps even emulate it in their marriage. And you can be sure they will tell your spouse what you say; such true rumors might make you a hero at home

*Refuse to tell risqué stories.*
Secular workplaces are often filled with suggestive stories and so-called cute jokes. Many people enjoy sharing those tidbits with their pastor. Though you probably won't wish to overreact when someone tells you a questionable story, refuse to pass it on. Establish and maintain a high standard for yourself.

*Speak up with prophetic outrage against sexual sins.*
Society has tried to soften adultery by calling it an affair or living together. But sexual sin is heinous and devastating, however benignly it is described. The sting is just as painful in family and in church as it has always been. It's time for each pastor in the land to

shout from the pulpit, "By God's grace and power, put a stop to such sin."

—H. B. L.

## Notes

1. *Newsweek* (July 9, 1997), n.p.
2. C. Peter Wagner, *Prayer Shield* (Ventura, CA: Regal Books, 1992), pp. 194, 195.

# hunger for power
## shrivels the soul

"I love the power but hate the travel," commented a church leader recently elected to the highest office in his family of churches.

Ecclesiastical power seekers love titles, expect to receive honor, exploit relationships, and are often willing to do almost anything to get more power. These toxic traits silently devour a leader's inner life. Yet these flaws are often accepted as the norm. Management specialist Peter Drucker sounds a lot like a prophet when he says, "Rank does not corner privilege or give power. It imposes responsibility."[1]

Greed for power, even when dressed in Sunday church clothes, is only a well-dressed rascal. Power junkies stifle churches. Their appetite can't be satisfied—they always want more. President John R. O'Neil of the California School of Professional Psychology exposes this issue when he observes, "Unlike the real nourishment of doing and producing, status and power are like sugar or cocaine, leaving the consumer ever hungrier for more."[2]

The sad secret no one wants to discuss is that churches of all sizes, all denominations and all geographic settings are repressed by misused power. Power addicts keep churches from breaking out to greatness in faith, service and compassion. Some controllers prefer to cripple, divide or kill a church, rather than welcome newcomers to positions of leadership.

Of course, God doesn't keep company with power addicts. His heart is grieved by their pragmatic expediency and exploitative moral shortcuts. As a consequence, churches led by power addicts do not experience the breakout blessing of God. These churches function by human energy and talent alone. Hundreds of churches are hanging on the ropes like a spent boxer. It is such a sad thing to see a power addict stifle a church and deprive a congregation of the tender guidance of the Lord. Sometimes, even when attendance losses and changing neighborhoods seem to be the reason for decline, the real problem may indeed be a lay leader or a pastor who is trying to wrest God's control away from Him.

A leader addicted to power:

1. Assumes that the ministerial position gives superior intelligence or spirituality
2. Allows personal attitudes and actions that do not square with the teachings of our Lord
3. Expects and accepts favored status
4. Forgets that ultimate accountability is to God
5. Believes people are following, when they are merely tolerating leadership
6. Holds authority and power, but refuses to use it for the good of the church
7. Is afraid to pray, "Is my leadership pleasing to the Lord Jesus?"

Power by its nature creates subtle temptations. Since ministers are usually chosen by the congregation and often serve on every key committee in the church, it's easy for them to think their control produces church health and growth. To make matters even more snarled, they are usually given free rein to operate the church as they see fit. Thus, it is possible for pastors to come to believe they know more than anyone else or to view themselves as the most Christ-motivated person in the congregation.

Some research done on smaller churches implies that dual factors keep congregations from growing. The first factor is an overly controlling pastor. In this case, the church cannot add more members or new programs because his span of control has already reached its limit. The second factor is the power grip of a lay leader who refuses to allow anything in the church to take place without his or her domination. Sadly, many pastors who most resent lay power controllers act in similar ways when they come into positions of power themselves.

There are several ways for pastors to misuse power in the church. If you are courageous enough to recognize that you have a power problem, you can begin to change your attitude and your behavior. Consider the following possibilities:

*Resist infallibility.*
Election, seniority or status does not produce infallibility. If you are tempted to think you know almost everything and that you make almost no mistakes, remember humility is a trait God honors. Thomas Mann's comical statement shows how silly infallibility is: "The good Lord sees your heart, not the braid on your jacket; before him we are all in our birthday suits, admirals and common men alike."[3]

*Avoid ownership obsessions.*
Power abusers love to talk about *my* church, *my* people, *my* sermon. In actuality, no human being owns any of those things. They are all God's. Our temptation to claim ownership must be constantly measured against the words of Jesus: "You know that the rulers of the Gentiles lord it over them, and their high officials exer-

cise authority over them. *Not so with you.* Instead, whoever wants to become great among you must be your servant, and whoever wants to be first must be your slave" (Matt. 20:25-27, italics added).

### Personify integrity.

Authenticity and integrity are not insignias stitched on the Sunday suit to create a good impression. Rather, they are an outflow of a pastor's devotion to the Chief. Bible scholar William Barclay once wrote this biting sentence: "Any religion which begets ostentation in action and pride in the heart is false religion."[4]

### Avoid arrogance.

Paul believes humility comes from an accurate memory of who we used to be: "Brothers, think of what you were when you were called. Not many of you were wise by human standards; not many were influential; not many were of noble birth. But God chose the foolish things of the world to shame the wise; God chose the weak things of the world to shame the strong. . . . It is because of him that you are in Christ Jesus, who has become for us wisdom from God—that is, our righteousness, holiness and redemption. Therefore, as it is written: 'Let him who boasts boast in the Lord' " (1 Cor. 1:26,27,30,31). The passage makes its own application to the contemporary Church.

### Welcome accountability.

Try creating an accountable relationship with peers and subordinates for use of your time, effectiveness, competency and personal spiritual development. As a result, you will grow personally and encourage others to increase their accountability. There is nothing like a truly humble leader to inspire confidence, hope and respect in members of their church. Jesus Himself said He came to serve, not to be served.

Test your use of power against Steven Mitchell's paraphrase of Psalm 15:

> Lord, who can be trusted with power,
>     And who may act in your place?
> Those with a passion for justice,
>     who speak the truth from their hearts;
> who have let go of selfish interests
>     and grown beyond their own lives;
> who see the wretched as their family
>     and the poor as their flesh and blood.
> They alone are impartial
>     and worthy of the people's trust.
> Their compassion lights up the whole earth,
>     and their kindness endures forever.[5]

The apostle Paul uses a short sentence of only six short words to summarize what he believes about power and its use: "Strength is for service, not status" (Rom. 15:1, *THE MESSAGE*).

—N. B. W.

### Notes

1. Peter Drucker, Quotable Quotes, *Reader's Digest* (August 1994), p. 9.
2. John R. O'Neil, *The Paradox of Success* (New York: C. P. Putnam's Sons, 1993), p. 87.
3. Rhonda Tripp, ed., *International Thesaurus of Quotations* (New York: Harper

and Row, 1970), p. 774.

4. William Barclay, *The Gospel of Matthew* (Philadelphia, PA: Westminster Press, 1958), p. 318.

5. Stephen Mitchell, *A Book of Psalms* (New York: HarperCollins, 1993), p. 7.

# the pastoral perspective on abortion

It started out as any ordinary Sunday morning—maybe even better than ordinary. The music was especially inspiring, the Scriptures were read with power and were focused on the theme of the service, and I thought my sermon was outstanding—maybe even dynamite (just kidding). I knew it was acceptable when so many parishioners stroked my ego at the door with comments like, "God used you today. Thanks for your courageous stand against abortion."

That's what many said, and I enjoyed their affirmation. I admired their courage because they supported me so completely. I felt very good about myself that day because I had been an enthusiastic spokesman for God on a controversial subject. The reactions were so positive that I made a mental note to preach on the abortion theme more often.

All this happened a long time ago before I knew much about abortion or the tragic lifelong consequences it causes.

In my impassioned message, I reminded my congregation how terrible abortion is. I gave them figures about how many millions of unborn children die each year. I went on and on, even repeating several of my points. I felt smug and satisfied.

After receiving what Dr. E. V. Hill calls "all the hugs and kisses" at the door, I went to my study as I did following every service. It was my practice to take a few minutes to unwind, to greet people at the door, to make a few notes about parishioners I needed to follow up on and to get ready to join my family for Sunday lunch.

Then came a knock. I opened the office door to find a young woman in her late 20s. I could tell she was troubled as she quietly said, "Pastor, I know you're tired, and I don't want to keep you. But could you spare a few minutes?" And I said, "Sure."

To be perfectly candid, I expected more affirmation. I thought she might say that the sermon on abortion was helpful or say, "I'm so glad you're my pastor."

But she greatly surprised me with her question: "Pastor, do you know how many women like me were sitting in the congregation today?" I thought she was talking about the number of women who came to church alone. I was clueless as to her real message.

She said, "Sorry, I am not expressing myself very well. What I really want to know is do you know how many women in the congregation are like me?"

Then I had to answer, "No, I really don't. I don't think I know what you mean."

Then like a broken dam at flood tide, she told me about the pain she felt from her own abortion. She graphically shared her sense of loss. She explained the agony she felt every anniversary that recalled the death of her unborn child. She told me how old her son would be by this time. She described how far from God she felt. Then she shocked me even more by saying that perhaps 1 in 10 women in her age group had had an abortion and that probably some of them were sitting in the pews of the church during my sermon that very morning.

She continued with indescribable emotion, "Today you didn't seem to show any mercy for women like me. Is there any hope? You seemed so determined to communicate your pro-life message that you forgot about women like me who have lived through an abortion. You failed to realize that many men also feel guilty because they insisted or at least consented to an abortion by their girlfriends or wives. For me, I felt I was dying by inches each time you uttered the word 'abortion.' "

That woman changed my life. She opened my eyes. She brought me back to the reality in which all pastors work—learning to hate sin more and learning to love sinners to a forgiveness only Christ provides. But sinners can't feel our love until we lower our voices to speak a word of compassion and offer pastoral support for those who have taken the wrong turn.

Let me say it again. I am pro-life. I am against abortion with every fiber of my being. But I am a pastor. And being a pastor places unique demands on my attitudes and actions.

To you pastors and church leaders who stand on the corners with pro-life signs as I have, who pray in front of abortion clinics as I have, who have pro-life organizations in your churches as I have—I commend you for your opposition to abortion. I respect your bravery and your courage. I laud you for taking a strong stand against this evil.

But I plead with you to also think about all the women who are spiritually traumatized when we preach about life issues because they have firsthand experience of this pain and loss. If you could feel my heart and hear my prayer just now, it would be, "God, forgive me for taking advantage of my pulpit when I was insensitive to hurting men and women whom You love. Forgive me when I hurt those who are already dying inside because of the sin of their past."

And pastors, I beg you, the next time you preach and teach on the subject of abortion—or any sin, for that matter—tell your congregation that sin is wrong, but don't forget to tell them that God offers forgiveness for those who live under the dark shadow of guilt. There is hope.

When you raise your voice to speak with such tenacious authority about the evils of abortion, be sure to lower that same voice to speak with quiet compassion to those who have been damaged by sin, assuring them there is healing, forgiveness and mercy. Tell them God loves them and cares for them. Tell them about God's pardon for sin. Tell them that coming to God is the answer to the crushing anguish they carry. Tell them that they do not need to carry this burden any longer.

Let's take seriously those incredible words of Scripture from Jesus' conversation with the woman taken in adultery: "Neither do I condemn you . . . Go now and leave your life of sin" (John 8:11).

Here are five simple ways to cultivate a deeper sensitivity to those who are dealing with the consequences of their sins and who question whether the church is willing to accept them:

*Add gentleness to preaching.*
Never preach against abortion without a tear in your eye. A veteran minister who had been a pastor for nearly a lifetime said, "I never deal with any sin without getting a tear in my eye. A tear of sadness for the consequences I see in the sinner's life. A tear of joy that no sin is too great for the Savior to forgive. And a tear that God, by grace, kept me from the same sin."

*Show sinners love as you warn against sin.*
Carefully find your way between being a prophet who denounces sin and a pastor who loves sinners. Most sinners know they have sinned; they need salvation and solutions rather than more condemnation. A balance is

needed and is not always easy to find. An authentic pastor is never easy on sin but always offers God's loving forgiveness to a sinner.

*Keep your preaching authentic.*
Caution—try never to use your pulpit to even a score with anyone. If you disregard this friendly advice, problems may flourish like weeds.

Remember, you may not have the whole story. Remember, people you are trying to win may resent a public discussion of their need. Remember, fair-minded believers may think you less than courageous for not personally approaching the individual whose sins you are denouncing. One old-time Christian told his pastor after a sermon that vehemently opposed the use of alcohol, "That sure was a powerful sermon for a hundred people in our church who have never taken a drink of the devil's brew in their lives."

Listen to your message through the ears of the most needy in your congregation. Do you offer hope? Do you communicate Christ's boundless love for sinners? I am not advocating that you tone down the gospel but that you speak in loving language your hearers will understand. Speak so they know you have spent time thinking through things from their perspective.

*Explore new ministries to care for unwed mothers and their babies.*
Lead your church to take positive action to care for children, to provide adoption as an alternative to abortion or to help a young mother or couple raise a child. There is a growing conviction, and a healthy concern, among

many Christians that the church should be prepared to help raise the child whose parents think an abortion is the only solution.

*View yourself as a physician of the soul.*
There was a time that pastoral care was given to everyone in need, both inside and outside the church, because the pastor was seen as a healer of the soul—a physician of the inner person. When someone opens up to you about a sin in their past, offer them whatever attention is needed for them to become whole in Christ. And it will make you a first row participant in the grace of God applied to the pains of human need.

—H. B. L.

# lonely but never alone

I often feel lonely; and whenever I preach on the subject of loneliness, I discover that many worshipers also feel alone. Most pastors know what I am speaking about.

I felt a terrible loneliness when I was dismissed from college in my sophomore year. My roommate sat on his bed crying—I've always wondered whether he was crying for me or crying because he would have to find another roommate. That day I placed all my possessions in a little box and walked out into uncertainty. I got into my car, not knowing where I was going. I felt as if nobody cared. Like the prodigal, I wanted to go to the far country, but I was afraid. You know the feeling: afraid to start but embarrassed to stay.

How could I go home? My parents would be disappointed. I had wasted their money. I had blown opportunities for sports, music, student leadership and an education. I had betrayed them and felt guilty and miserable about it. I felt that all that mattered was gone.

Another dreadfully bleak moment of loneliness came when my dad died. When I received the call that he had passed, I went to his room. I stood alone next to his body and realized that I was truly an orphan. As an only child, I didn't know whom to call, what to do or how to act. Beverley came to the hospital as soon as she could. But I felt so alone. So many times since that day, I have reached for the phone just to say, "Hey, Dad, how's it going?" only to pull my hand away. There would be no more phone calls. He wasn't there. My dad was gone.

Now I realize that loneliness is not always as dramatic as being dismissed from college or losing your father in death. But the pain of loneliness always hurts.

It may come after you have preached a poor sermon. You have taken 30 minutes of everyone's time, and you have not done justice to the Lord's Word.

It may come when you realize you have not been a good marriage partner. You've argued about something senseless with your spouse. You've caused pain or chaos. You know you, as a pastor, are supposed to have the answers for building a good marriage, but you can't get it right yourself.

Maybe you feel lonely when you have invested incredible amounts of energy in counseling a couple. You loved them and gave them time. Over and over again, you have been there for them. Then they walk away, as though you do not exist. Loneliness comes to a pastor at times of disappointment, betrayal and rejection.

Oddly enough, it is sometimes the high moments that make me feel lonely. It's hard to explain why. When the sermon has gone well, you want to tell someone. You feel like shouting from the housetop, "Man, look what I did. I just hit a home run for Jesus!" But as you realize that most everyone is too busy to share your victory, loneliness sweeps over you.

Though loneliness has many causes and is quite common among ministers, it can be terrifying. Ann Landers credits Eugene Kennedy with this advice which always works for me: "When a person asks that age-old question, 'What can I do about my terrible loneliness?' the best answer is still, 'Do something for somebody else.' "[1] What a positive driving force that is for Christian service.

The best remedies for loneliness are rooted in relationships. Your relationship with the Lord is most important. That contact keeps you open and honest and aboveboard so you never have to hide from God.

Colleagues are another remedy for loneliness. Find someone who loves you, accepts you and understands you. Let them see your heart for ministry. Then give them permission to ask hard questions about your inner world.

Family can also help us with bouts of loneliness. Affirm your love for them. Let them know how much you need them and how much you count on their support and love.

I sometimes think how lonely Jesus must have felt. After all, no one had ever been through His experience. It was unique in all history. His disciples couldn't relieve His loneliness; they couldn't even stay awake to be there for Him in His hour of agony and despair. What's more, He knew that the one person who did understand Him was about to turn His back on Him. Yet what did Jesus do to relieve His loneliness? Party? Spend money? Talk a lot? No, He often withdrew to a quiet place to be alone. Oddly enough, loneliness is sometimes cured by truly being alone with the Father; by absorbing His love in quiet solitude, pouring out our needs to Him and thanking Him that because Jesus bore the ultimate loneliness, we are never totally alone.

Think about the great remedy found in relationship to Christ. Build on His wonderful promise, "Lo, I am with you always, even to the end of the age" (Matt. 28:20, *NASB*). Deepening fellowship with the Lord is the answer. I get strength from the scriptural promise that God sent the Holy Spirit into our lives—the Paraclete, the One who comes alongside.

The gospel song from my childhood, "How Can I Be Lonely?" runs through my mind. The verse that encourages me most about ministry says, "In the hour of sad bereavement or of bitter loss, I find support and consolation at the Cross. Want or woe or suffer-

ing, all seem glorified when He daily walks and talks with me."
And the chorus lifts this true-to-life refrain, "How can I be lonely
when I've Jesus only to be my companion and unfailing Guide?"[2]
How can a pastor reduce or take advantage of loneliness?

### Accept loneliness as a part of living.

Often your feelings of isolation can be reduced by helping parishioners or staff members work through their
loneliness. To accept loneliness as part of the human
experience puts you in touch with many people. Pastors
are never completely destitute as long as there is someone who trusts and accepts them.

### Differentiate between solitude and loneliness.

The devotional masters make the point that solitude is
needed in ministry to keep us connected to the Father.
They are right. Quiet times alone with God enrich our
ministry and illuminate our outlook. In her 1965 book
*Mrs. Steven Hears the Mermaids Singing*, May Sarton says,
"Loneliness is the poverty of self; solitude is the richness
of self."[3]

### Cross-examine your loneliness.

Take stock of how many love you and depend on you.
Someone said, "Loneliness starts with terrible blind-
ness." And that's often truer than we care to admit.
Remember when Elijah complained to God, "The
Israelites have rejected your covenant, broken down your
altars, and put your prophets to death with the sword. I
am the only one left, and now they are trying to kill me
too" (1 Kings 19:10). Haven't you made a similar speech
to God: "I am the only one left." I know I have.

Then God jolts Elijah with a solid dose of reality: "Yet I reserve seven thousand in Israel—all whose knees have not bowed down to Baal" (1 Kings 19:18).

*Realize loneliness may result from misused power.*
The high and mighty are sometimes lonely because they think it is beneath their status to associate with common folks. Joseph Newton realized this possibility when he wrote, "People are lonely because they build walls instead of bridges."[4] Misused power often frightens parishioners right out of our lives. By our controlling spirits and aloofness, we deprive ourselves of the company we need to alleviate our loneliness.

*Clarify your perspective.*
I question myself about loneliness—why am I feeling the way I feel? Loneliness is something rooted in our confusing concepts about love. I always profit from Dag Hammarskjöld's advice: "Pray that your loneliness may spur you into finding something to live for, great enough to die for."[5]

It is also useful in a discussion of cultivating a clear perspective about loneliness to consider Bernard M. Martin's insightful sentence: "Loneliness is the very thing which God has chosen to be one of the schools of training for His very own. It is the fire that sheds the dross and reveals the gold."[6]

—H. B. L.

**Notes**
1. William Safir and Leonard Safir, comp., *Good Advice* (New York: Wings

Books, 1982), p. 205.

2. Haldor Lillenas, *Praise and Worship* (Kansas City, MO: Nazarene Publishing House, 1928), p. 155.

3. Rebecca Davis and Susan Mesner, eds., *The Treasury of Religious and Spiritual Quotations* (Pleasantville, NY: Readers Digest Association, 1994) p. 302.

4. Ted Goodman, ed., *The Forbes Book of Business Quotations* (New York: Black Dog and Leventhal Publishers, 1997), p. 538.

5. Safir and Safir, *Good Advice*, p. 205.

6. Goodman, *The Forbes Book of Business Quotations,* p. 538.

# don't become
# a castaway

Recently in a question-and-answer session with pastors, I was asked how I would prepare and mentor a staff person for effective service in the church. It had been noted that the average term of a staff associate is less than two years—just not long enough.

Two things came to mind immediately about mentoring and preparing. The Christian faith requires a radical personal encounter with the Lord. And this faith of ours must grow across a lifetime of devoted obedience to Christ. Every staff member must know both those realities personally.

It is a sad fact that some staff members—even senior pastors—have never really committed to a called life. Some of them have a notion of paid, secular jobs, rather than a life of ministry. Christians in staff positions, though they have been born again, sometimes fail to discover the adventure of lifelong obedience to Christ. Some lose their way spiritually because they handle holy issues so routinely and become so involved in the needs of others that they do not keep themselves spiritually healthy for the work of the gospel. That happens most often when the life-transforming work of Christ is allowed to become ordinary or commonplace. It is likely to happen when the miraculous attractiveness of Jesus is allowed to grow dim.

Strange as it sounds, it's easy for us to neglect cultivating the roots of faith in ourselves that we try so hard to develop in others. Thus, while developing others, we can risk becoming castaways. Such staff members may have a form of godliness, without its power. In this downward spiral, we give up so much to gain so little.

One of my greatest disappointments began when I invited a young seminary graduate and his wife to join our staff. He was an incredible youth specialist, something like a Pied Piper with teens. I have never known anyone with as much charisma to attract young people. As this young minister began his work in our church, it appeared he would lead our youth in a very mature manner, rather than merely offer them a busy activity schedule. Every pastor would appreciate that kind of youth ministry, and I was no exception.

Sadly, a tragedy soon set in. Being still inexperienced myself as a senior pastor, I was not aware of danger signals, and no doubt I did not mentor him as I should have. Though he was married to a beautiful young lady and had fathered their child, it soon became apparent that he was a practicing homosexual. He blew his cover by making advances toward a teen boy in the church. The parents were livid, as you might expect. The evidence was conclusive. I had to deal with the issue, but I was heartsick. I dismissed him and tried to help him find secular employment in another state. I did everything I could to salvage his marriage, but it didn't work. The paralyzing sadness this incident caused throughout our congregation is difficult to describe.

For him, the losses were even more painful. He finally died an agonizing death as a consequence of AIDS. Over time, he partnered with many men who carried the virus that finally killed him. His spiritual decline started as a devilish waste of potential. All this was so heartbreaking, so irrational, so contrary to God's plan for this man, his family and our church.

The last time I saw him was the day I officiated at his son's wedding. He was older now and very sick. The wages of his sins were so sad and so unnecessary. How can it be calculated what might have been his gigantic influence and satisfaction in service if he had kept his heart right toward the Lord?

Another young man served with me right out of college. He was a handsome athlete who had an opportunity to try out for a professional baseball team. He was powerfully built, winsome and faithful. Though his family background was not ideal—his mother died when he was young and his father traveled away from home every week in his work—he seemed to be a settled Christian.

The young man served teens in our church with distinction. I was proud he was on our staff team. He stayed on at the church after I moved to another assignment, but soon his life began to unravel. He started to lie and to steal. For no apparent reason, he broke into stores, taking items he could easily afford to purchase for himself. He was taken to trial, found guilty and sentenced to several years in prison. I remember receiving his heartrending letter from jail. He realized he would never be able to minister again. He knew the consequences of his actions had a much larger price than he had expected to pay. Fortunately, his loving wife is still by his side.

What could we have done to make his life different? Or perhaps a more appropriate question is, What could he have done to make his life different?

I believe his story teaches that every Christian worker has split-second decisions to make when tempted. A negative choice colors life forever. In our own setting of service, each of us walks a fine line between good and evil that may sometimes take us pretty near an abyss. There is much we can do to avoid getting too close to the line.

Let's be realistic—the world and its values pressure us intensely. Though we do not need to fall, we can. And all around us our colleagues sometimes do.

My reason for sharing these stories is to show how one can be near holy things without being holy. It is possible to preach about forgiveness and not forgive. Even a pastor or staff member can have such a flawed value system that makes wrong seem right. Ministers can give so much effort to ministry that they neglect their soul's health. Pastoral leaders can become so professional in dealing with people that they forget they are not CEOs, but rather God's representatives of peace, grace and tough love. Church leaders can be so focused on getting a crowd or building a strong institution that they forget a church must be centered on Christ and not on their own agendas. It is easy to run on empty and become cynical, bitter, stubborn and self-centered—only to destroy one's self by making a huge mistake.

If you want to avoid becoming a castaway and to prevent such failures in your staff members, try some of these adventuresome suggestions:

*Live what you preach.*
Never preach until you are prepared to apply every line of your sermon to yourself. If you have unhealthy or unbridled personal issues and you do not get deliverance, those issues will ruin your ministry in the end. When you stand before your people, you must be able to sing, "It is well with my soul."

*Commit to spiritual self-care.*
A physician may be a good doctor without being healthy. But a pastor cannot meet the spiritual needs of others without being spiritually balanced and healthy. Ministry requires us to show the way home to God.

*Mentor staff. Take your mentoring task seriously.*

Those who are on staff with you should become your spiritual children. Just as you take responsibility for making yourself spiritually accountable to a trusted colleague, offer to provide the same accountability for someone else.

*Lead the way.*

Speak often with other staff members about what God is doing in your life. Tell them what burdens you in your prayer life. Ask them to share insights God is giving them from Scripture. Seek to be the spiritual leader of staff members so they are fully convinced they have a pastor rather than a boss, one they can count on in every situation.

*Humble yourself.*

Humility is a spiritual quality that becomes more effective with use. Too many pastors lead their staffs as if they were presidents of a college, hospital, bank or department store. That doesn't work. The ideal relationship between pastor, staff and volunteers is one of servant leadership where Jesus is the model rather than Peter Drucker. Whenever you are tempted to pull rank on those whom you lead, ask the Lord to take you back to the upper room where He took the form of a servant— that's what He wants from every pastor. And that is what every staff member needs from their senior pastor.

*Grow past your disappointments.*

After I invested myself in someone, I experienced heartbreak when they failed to prove trustworthy. That's especially true with staff members. You remember that when Demas deserted Paul because "he loved this world" (2 Tim. 4:10), the apostle went on with his ministry. As a pastor, your role is to read the signs. Do not be afraid to stand in the gap and confront those you see walking down a trail that could lead to destruction. I think that is what "shepherd the flock" means (1 Pet. 5:2, *NASB*).

*Teach staff to value their influence.*
The influence of the young ministers I discussed earlier was enormous. In God's grace, some of their influence was positive, so that some teens they served are now lay leaders in that same church. But a stain of sin and carelessness remains. That sin not only cost them their ministry, but it turned some teens and parents away from the Lord forever.

—H. B. L.

# you are not always in control

The plane I was flying on was being hijacked, and I was only a few feet from the frightening action. As I sat petrified in my seat, I prayed that it would end peacefully and quickly. To this day, I still pray that I never have to experience anything like it again.

My plan was to meet my family for a vacation in Palm Springs, California. The first part of the journey was a nonstop flight on United Airlines from Portland, Oregon, to Los Angeles. The gate personnel offered me a seat in first class, which I accepted happily—perhaps because they were overbooked. After we were well on our way to Los Angeles, I noticed several flight attendants giving their undivided attention to a man who had come into the first-class cabin holding his stomach as if he were in pain. They gathered around him and even had him sitting on the jump seat. Because of their intense concern, I thought he was ill.

When you fly a lot, you are accustomed to unusual circumstances sometimes taking place, so I didn't think too much about what was happening. All this activity seemed like a minor disturbance until the pilot announced, "There's a gentleman on board who does not wish to land in Los Angeles, and we plan to accommodate him." Wow—what I thought was an insignificant problem had suddenly become a frightening event, and I was in the middle of it. My seat was less than 10 feet from the hijacker's seat during most of the flight. In spite of all those moments you have, thinking what you would do in an emergency, when something like this happens, believe me, you will experience no burning desire to become a hero.

The pilot circled a few times, then headed toward Northern California. We landed in a remote area of the airport near San Jose and then took off again and landed in another city. Sometime later we landed back at our point of embarkment in Portland, Oregon. The trip ended there, when the hijacker surrendered. It had been an all-night flight to nowhere.

Later we learned that he had murdered his father when he was 13 and had served time in state institutions. He had recently violated his parole and knew that he was going back to a prison. By hijacking a plane, which is a federal offense, he thought he could be incarcerated in a federal penitentiary. I am not sure why—maybe he thought the accommodations were better and the jailers more pleasant. Who knows, but he did get his wish—a 40-year sentence.

After it was all over, I reflected on what had happened to me and to the other passengers. There were no heroic actions; nor was there a sense of panic. Obviously, the hijacker wanted to be in control, so we were happy to let him have it his way. We even had to ask for his permission to use the lavatory. But when we landed in Portland, the hijacker was ready to surrender.

The issue of who was in control changed quickly after we landed. The plane was immediately surrounded by a SWAT team, ready for any eventuality. Passengers were led off the plane by sections, starting at the back. Finally they allowed the first-class section to leave, followed by the flight attendants and pilots.

When I was allowed off the plane, reporters and news cameras were there. My picture and comments were splashed across the pages of our local paper. Though I was in the middle of this excitement, my family waiting in Southern California only knew the plane had been delayed. They had no clue as to the danger I was in.

As I look back on the incident, it seems more scary now than it was when the event happened. That day, God gave me great peace in the midst of an incredibly frightening situation.

The first reason I tell this story is because it has to do with a pastor's trust in the Lord Jesus. It is amazing how much peace God gives us even in crises if we simply rely on Him. In other words, let's practice what we preach.

The second reality is true both in my story and in my life as a pastor: I was completely out of control. At 32,000 feet, we were controlled by a hijacker who claimed to have a bomb strapped to his waist. To have tried to alter the situation would have made matters much worse. Though many of us become frustrated when we are out of control in some aspect of our lives, most of us are more out of our control than we realize.

Still another lesson came through to me loud and clear when I recognized how quickly unexpected events move into our lives. Crisis, delay, disappointment, illness and even death are experiences of life that tend to come at inconvenient times. Perhaps the test of our faith and the strength of our endurance come more in those moments of great surprise than when we are able to carefully calculate the events of living.

The lessons I want to share from this story concern a pastor's inner resources. Sometimes our people do not demonstrate the characteristics of Christ in the crisis and crunch because they do not see it in us. In too many places and situations, the Christian faith has become simply a subject to be discussed rather than a life to be lived every hour of every day. Let's change that in the thinking of the congregation God has given us to lead. Here's how:

*Get ready for storms.*

Stormy weather comes to the saint as well as the sinner. Dark valleys come to the pastor as well as the physician, banker or bricklayer. Get ready for storms. Get everything tied down. Get your faith cup filled to the top. One of my favorite assurances from Scripture for facing storms is "He is the faithful God, keeping his covenant of love to a thousand generations" (Deut. 7:9, *NIV*). I rejoice because that promise includes me.

*Trust is contagious.*

Allow your parishioners to grow in their understanding of God by watching how much you depend on Him in tough situations. Perhaps every pastor wants to serve in a quiet church that has few problems and pays a great salary. The catch is that those places are hard to find. The quiet, tranquil churches, if they exist, are few and far between because fevered, fretting pastors like us have produced churches like themselves. The good news is this: In nearly every congregation, whether in a boisterous or subdued setting, when Christians see a loving pastor who trusts God for every need, their confidence and dependence on the Lord increase. A foundation for a life of trust is this sure promise: "The One who called you is completely dependable. If he said it, he'll do it!" (1 Thess. 5:24, *THE MESSAGE*).

*Give priority to what matters.*

Building impressive church buildings or adding slick new programs often creates an impressive reputations, and we pastors begin to hear encouraging, positive conversations among our members. Such a response is enjoyably affirming for us. But God intended buildings and programs to be mere delivery systems for something much more lasting. The abiding issues like peace, trust, hope, assurance, love and faith are easy to overlook when we give too much attention to mortar and dollars. When we stand before God at the end of life, the list of abiding provisions of the gospel will have a much higher importance than constructions or money. Such priorities become extremely clear to us when we are thrown into crisis situations like being hijacked.

An acquaintance of mine was once driving to an oral exam in order to obtain his doctoral degree. He had his wife and ten-month-old baby in the car. On a rainy day, going about 55 miles an hour, he lost control of the car and hydroplaned. The car spun several times and then struck a guard rail and came to a halt, nose first into oncoming traffic. Although the young man and his wife were unhurt, when they climbed out of their car, they discovered to their horror that their baby had been thrown from the back of their hatchback and was nowhere to be found. By God's great mercy, that little girl, after flying through the air, landed in the only patch of soft grass anywhere nearby. She had only a slightly fractured leg. After settling his wife and baby with some friends who lived nearby, the young doctoral candidate went on to his oral exam, which he passed. But how differently he felt about that exam. So grateful was he to the Lord for saving his life and those of his wife and baby that the exam seemed like a game. That baby is now grown, with two children of her own, and is helping her pastor/husband do church planting in Berlin, Germany.

When we are suddenly faced with life-threatening

incidents over which we have no control and whose outcomes are anyone's guesses, we find ourselves face-to-face with the real things in life. It is then that we find strength in our faith in Christ, which abides forever.

*Christ owns the Church.*
The Church belongs to the Lord. He started it. He bought it. And He promised to build it.

A. W. Tozer calls pastors to victory over possessiveness. He uses Abraham and the test he endured of giving up his son Isaac. About Abraham, Tozer writes: "The old man of God lifted his head to respond to the Voice, and stood there on the mount strong and pure and grand, a man marked out by the Lord for special treatment, a friend and favorite of the Most High. Now he was a man wholly surrendered, a man utterly obedient, a man who possessed nothing."[1]

Tozer continues with an inspiring bottom line for contemporary pastors: "Yet was not this poor man rich? Everything he had owned before was still his to enjoy: sheep, camels, herds, and goods of every sort. He had also his wife and his friends, and best of all he had his son Isaac safe by his side. He had everything, but he possessed nothing. . . . There is the sweet theology of the heart which can be learned only in the school of renunciation."[2]

Victory over possessiveness sounds like an obligation, a duty or a responsibility—and it is. But there is something much more significant in this idea: when we relinquish control, God does much more with His Church through His people than we could ever do through possessiveness.

*Use crises to check your inner reserves.*

Maybe that sentence sounds too complicated. What I have in mind is that when you experience a crisis, whatever it is, that you would look deep into your heart to see what you find. In the process, check to see if the grace of the Lord Jesus is still at work there. Check to see if your inner resources are strong enough to sustain you and help you persevere when the tests, stresses and surprises come, as they will. But most of all, throw yourself once again on the grace of our Savior, realizing that it is through the power of His Holy Spirit that your heart and mind will be kept and that you will remain faithful, discarding the unimportant and delighting in our treasure, Jesus Christ.

—H. B. L.

**Notes**

1. A. W. Tozer, *The Pursuit of God* (Camp Hill, PA: Christian Publications, 1982), p. 27.
2. Ibid.

# the Minister

who

loves at

home

# the legacy you leave

Nearly every year, near the Reverand Billy Graham's birthday, a national magazine runs a feature story about him. A couple of years ago, *Parade* magazine asked Dr. Graham about the meaning of his life. As I recall, the editor questioned, "If you had your life to live over, what would you do differently?" Mr. Graham replied, "Three things: I'd study more, travel less and spend more time with my family."

The next question was, "How do you want to be remembered?" Graham answered without hesitation, "I want to be remembered as one who practiced what I preached." Interesting, isn't it? The most prominent minister of this century describing a legacy every pastor could easily leave—to be remembered as one who practiced what they preached.

I buried my dad in the London family plot in Oklahoma City a few years ago. I'll probably be buried there some day myself. As I walked around that small area of the cemetery, I stood by my grandfather's grave. A. S. London was a lay Sunday School evangelist who touched thousands. He relished life and spent enormous energy for the cause of Christ. He impacted me profoundly, for in a myriad ways he told me over and over, "I love you."

While in retirement, he would send me three or four letters a week. Interestingly enough, the letters had been written to him by others and he just sent them on to me. So he'd address those letters with a scrawling comment and then write "oodles" at the bottom of the page, which meant "lots of love." Then the word "Pop." To this day, I still think about his secondhand letters.

The last time I saw Pop, he was dying of leukemia in a Houston hospital. We both knew this would be the last time we would be together. I sat for hours on the side of his bed, just loving him. I remember asking him, "Pop, what has been the secret of your life? How have you been so effective?" He was so sick I didn't know if he could answer. But the hollow sockets of his eyes filled with tears as he put his big shaking hand into mine. This former hulk of a man now weighed slightly more than 100 pounds. With great effort he responded, "Junior, it's one thing for people to know how much God loves them, but it's another thing for them to know how much you really love them."

That was not so profound; but, you see, love was the lifeblood of my grandfather's ministry. Because of him, it has become the essence of my life and ministry. I want desperately to let my family and congregation know how much I love them. I want to say it over and over. Whatever I have to do or say, I am determined that love will be my legacy. I want my family and my church to know that I love them. I am prepared to make any sacrifice to be sure they know they are loved.

The legacy issue became especially important for me after my father died. As the only child in a family, it suddenly dawned on me that I had moved to another level of responsibility. I had become the custodian of the love that must be passed on to the next generation. And to my extended family and everyone I touch in ministry, I am trying to live and share Ephesians 3:16-19 (*THE MESSAGE*):

I ask him to strengthen you by his Spirit—not a brute strength but a glorious inner strength—that Christ will live in you as you open the door and invite him in. And I ask him that with both feet planted firmly on love, you'll be able to take in with all Christians the extravagant dimensions of Christ's love. Reach out and experience the breadth! Test its length! Plumb the depths! Rise to the heights! Live full lives, full in the fullness of God.

When you become the head of an extended family, you soon realize that much of who your family will become has a direct correlation to how you love them and how you care for them and how you pass on the essentials of life.

May I suggest a few ways to ensure that legacy:

*Check the love quotient.*
I heard a wonderful lay leader recently say, "Our new pastor is very gifted, but we do not know yet whether he loves us." The power of your legacy is determined by your love for those God has given you to serve and whether they know you love them.

*Learn from your influencers.*
Clarify your own experiences. Who most influenced and shaped your life and ministry? Was it technique, experience, competence or love? How do you measure their impact? I predict your list will be made up of loving people who believed in you.

*Keep the long view in mind.*
If you consider the things that break relationships, you discover most problems are rooted in current frustration and have little significance for a lifetime. Live by the idea that what troubles you will soon pass. That quiets your frustrations and undermines overly quick reactions.

*Express love.*

As you read this sentence, ask yourself who do you love that does not know it. Or who do you love that you expect to know it by osmosis. Pick up the phone. Write a note. Get on e-mail. Who needs to hear you say "I love you"?

*Do yourself a favor by loving others.*

Church folks who feel loved will overlook your faults. They will love you in return, sometimes in incredibly abundant measure. This is not manipulation but reality—those who love are loved.

*Write a spiritual will.*

Make a list of the spiritual qualities you want your church and family to remember about you. Put names next to the ideas. Then write in detail what these characteristics mean to you. Then pretend you are overlooking the banister of eternity at your own memorial service. What will those present say about your legacy? If your answer is what really matters to you, rejoice. If not, consider ways to develop or improve these characteristics in yourself.

—H. B. L.

# the model for the next generation

The day my dad died, I moved from Junior to patriarch. The awesome responsibility of now being the senior influencer to my grown children and my grandchildren hit me like a ton of bricks.

Junior was what my dad and granddad often called me, and I grew to dislike it immensely. Such a name was especially difficult to accept after I became a grown man with years of pastoral experience and adult children of my own. But after their promotion to heaven, it dawned on me that a mantle of responsibility for developing faith, stability, strength and influence for the next generation now rested heavily on my shoulders.

This responsibility means being the point man for the development of the ongoing value system of Christian faith in my family. Here's how it works. I used to be a follower, a son, a learner and a disciple in the London family; now the passing of generations in front of me makes me a leader, father, teacher and mentor. Everything I needed Dad and Granddad to be for me, the next generation now needs from me. That's an awesome reality and a troubling responsibility.

My dad lived to be 88. His last hospitalization was for a condition that no one thought was life threatening. He began to preach when he was 16 and continued as long as strength and opportunity allowed. He had many high points and quite a few low points that affected my life and ministry. I knew how much he influenced me, but I never realized the astounding impact he made on his world until people started writing to me after his death.

Dad taught me a lot about ministry, often in casual conversation. Some of his wise insights still guide my ministry. He used to tease me, "Junior, don't take yourself too seriously, because nobody else does." He simply wanted me to be free and to do my best, instead of moping around with a heaviness in my spirit. Another time he advised, "Don't preach long sermons." In an era when preaching giants spoke for 50 minutes, he never preached for more than 25. But people regularly responded to the gospel through his preaching. Another time he suggested: "Son, use a lot of humor. Let people laugh at themselves or you, but let them laugh. Life is serious enough, so don't browbeat them. Don't beat them up. Let them be happy in Christ." He also told me many times to preach with a clear connection to Jesus Christ: "Make sure that when people have heard your message, they have seen themselves in God's looking glass—and that when the message is over, they will have seen Jesus, and in seeing Jesus, they have seen themselves in relationship to Him."

You may not yet feel the weight of this responsibility. But one day, you will move from being a junior to assuming the role of mentor or patriarch for the next generation. It can happen so quickly. Be ready and do it well.

On the day Dad died, the hospital called me at my office in Colorado Springs shortly after I had been to visit him. They told me he had taken a turn for the worse and urged me to come back. When I arrived at the hospital, he was already gone. The doctor asked if I would like to spend a few minutes alone with Dad. So I walked in, closed the door and cried. It was an emotional, life-defining moment for me, his only child.

Please don't think me discourteous to my father's memory, but as I looked down at his body on that hospital bed, I thought, "You were a great dad, but not a very good father." He was often gone when I needed him; his ministry took him away from me much of the time. Though I never lacked for anything he could provide, I never really *had* him. I feel sad about that for myself and for our family, but I cannot change that.

Those moments in the hospital room, as I sorted through my grief-stricken emotions, clarified that sense of moving up a notch. Now that I was first generation, there were no more excuses. I couldn't compromise my behavior because of my dad's shortcomings. I couldn't be a victim anymore. It was my turn to be an example, a model for the next generation. The incredible sense of awe that I felt made my soul soften toward my dad. My disappointments about the things he may not have done so well melted away. I felt humility and a sense of tender forgiveness toward my dad. And I turned from that room with a sense of utter dependence on the power of God. "Help me to communicate Your love and Your gospel to them," I prayed.

My challenge to every pastor is: Be a great parent and an example to those who look to you. But how?

### View faith as intergenerational.

Rejoice when the next generation and their children embrace all you believe about God and the future. But when they don't, be sure not to reject them. Find common ground. Many adults who have rejected the faith of their childhood begin to start back to a meaningful connection with God when their children are born or when they realize that their parents, their own bulwarks of faith, will not be around forever as a source of spiritual help. Cultivate and cherish a mature parental friendship with your grown children.

### See ministry and parenting as mutually supportive.

The secret is to think of ministry as a way of life that

allows plenty of room for family. When ministry is viewed as a job, the children always wonder why their parent gives so much time to the church. Use creativity to tie church and family together in a mutuality that blesses both.

*Profit from mistakes of former generations.*
Although they had good intentions, many ministers in other generations mistakenly believed they had to sacrifice family on the altar of ministry. Instead of following in the ruts cut by their blunders, let's ask God to help us trace new tracks. Let's learn to use their errors as stepping stones to make life a holy, winsome adventure, without destroying either family or ministry.

*Forgive your parents' mistakes.*
Most of our godly parents did the best they could with what they knew. Of course they struggled with pains from their past. Who among us can claim to be free of such troubles? However, we are sometimes blind to our own mistakes because we can't get past our childhood hurts. If you are shackled by the past, ask Christ to renew a spirit of forgiveness toward your parents for their mistakes. When you are free from the burdens of the past, you will see before you a shining world of opportunity—where your own children and grandchildren are waiting to go out on a walk by your side and to learn from your love and wisdom.

*Never underestimate your impact on the next generation.*
Think back over your own life. Do you remember the smile on that first-grade teacher's face when she first

taught you to read? Do you remember the sense of joy you got from that basketball coach's affirming comment? Bring to mind those moments when someone special in your life said a word or did something for you that you will never forget. They may have been unaware of the effect they had on you. Don't forget that those around you need the same sense of encouragement. They need you to say those nice thoughts you have about them and to come to the birthday party, even if you don't enjoy the cake, and the noise is a bit much for you. They need to know that you are on their side. I once knew an elderly, deaf preacher who attended services each time church doors were open. When asked why he came when he couldn't hear a thing, he replied, "I just want everybody to know which side I am on." And they did, too.

—H. B. L.

# loving best the most important people

Everybody makes mistakes in parenting. Remorse often sets in, sometimes years later, when we think how much better we could have been—if we had only known how. Sadly, children do not come equipped with instruction manuals.

However, kids are so responsive to love that they overlook mistakes in parenting if they know how much we care for them and if they see us sincerely putting their interests first. One woman with eight children was once comforting her grown daughter, who was terribly distraught that she had lost her temper with her three-year-old. "But, darling," said the mother, "surely you remember all the times I lost my temper with some of you." The daughter, slightly calmed by now, replied, "No, Mom. The only thing I remember was opening your bedroom door one day to see you on your knees by your bed, praying out loud for me." God is gracious to us parents and often wipes the bad memories from our children's memories.

As I have mentioned, I was an only child. I learned my parenting skills from an absentee father and a devoted mother. I was also greatly influenced as a boy by my cousin, Dr. James Dobson, and the way his family loved and cared for one another. He was like a brother to me, and still is. Regrettably, I was a parent before he became so knowledgeable, so I was not able to glean as much guidance from him as I could have, had he been born 10 years earlier.

Though I am not sure where it came from, there was an unusual push for perfection in my family. Apparently, I helped carry it to the next generation. When we were in our first church, Brad, my son, was doing especially well in the public school right across the street. He enjoyed school and thrived on our affirmation of his success. He was learning to write, and he was particularly good at spelling. For several weeks, much to our delight, he brought home perfect spelling tests.

One day, he didn't come home from school. Darkness had begun to set in, and Beverley was worried. So I went looking for him. I found him sitting on one of those outdoor corridors many California schools have. He had been crying—his eyes were swollen and red.

I was angry. I went through the usual list. In a gruff voice, I asked him, "What are you doing here? Didn't you realize we'd be worried sick about you?" It was a big load for such a little boy. Then Brad said, "Dad, I was afraid to come home because I missed some spelling words today. I was sure you would be mad at me." We had been so foolish. In Brad's mind, our affirmation had become a parental demand for perfection. He thought that since he was a pastor's kid, I expected him to be better than others. I don't think I ever really believed that—but that is what Brad heard in his head.

The mistakes we pastors make with our children are often the same ones any parent makes. But there are some mistakes that are particularly devastating for PKs (preacher's kids). We imply, or sometimes say, "You have to set an example because you are the pastor's kids. You have to be quiet in church. You must sit still. You can never embarrass your father or mother." Sometimes we are surprised to hear ourselves say, "You have to be a role model so other children will know how to act in the house of God." Isn't it hilarious to think a six- or seven-year-old knows what a role model is? When you stop to think about it, it's absurd to make children believe they have to measure up to some behavior standard because they were born to a parsonage family. And the more unrealistic our expectations, the more likely the children will be to shut us out of their lives when they get a little older.

In most churches the congregation expects the pastor's children to be themselves—normal kids. And most of the time they live up to that expectation. Our goal for all the children of the church should be the same one we hold for our own children: to become all they can be for God.

My few minutes with Brad on the way home from school that day taught me a huge lesson. I started to see more clearly the kinds of pressures that I had put on him. Sometimes the pressures were indirect or subtle, but they were pressures nonetheless. I wish I could say that I was forever guided by what I discovered that day. But I didn't always practice what I learned. Sometimes I went back to the old way of telling my boys, "You are the pastor's sons, and I count on you to do your best." That's too much to expect.

Being friends with my grown children is one of life's finest blessings. I am a most fortunate father. Brad and Bryan have grown up to be wonderful men of God. They are better fathers than I ever was. They are sensitive family men. They are amazing trophies of grace. And their development is a testimony to what God can help a clergy couple do in their parenting. If I could only take back some of those earlier years.

One of my greatest pleasures whenever I am with my sons is to observe how much they love each other and enjoy being together. I know they are serving the Lord; that produces great satisfaction. To know they are bringing their own families up in close relationship to Jesus is a gift I cherish.

But I know some of you are grief stricken, because your grown children are not serving the Lord. And so you suffer anguish when you see them ignore the faith values you taught them. You pray that they will not throw away the priceless treasures of their heritage.

And so you lie awake going over what you might have done differently. You cry out in prayer during the night hours. "Other parents have made mistakes, too," you argue with God. "Sometimes I didn't know what to do. I did my best. I loved them." But your conscience haunts you. You didn't spend enough time with them. You didn't go to that basketball game you promised to attend. You neglected to read the Bible and pray with them as much as you should have.

Take courage. There is hope. I want to remind every pastor and spouse that God is not through with your children. No matter how old they are, they are still *your* children. And you can still do some parenting. That quiet inner strength that only a stalwart Christian communicates has far more impact on them than you imagine. Rest in the knowledge that God is at work in their memories because of what they learned from you. Believe it and feed your faith on that fact.

Also remember that God has many ways to reach them, in addition to what you can do. I once read of the granddaughter of a Welsh pastor, whose parents had seemingly no interest in the faith. The girl went to her grandpa's church until she was eight, and then she turned away from the faith. She began living the fast life and finally went on a lark to France, where she became pregnant, had an abortion, became pregnant again and gave birth to a deaf son. Susan's grandfather had prayed for years for her, but when he died, she was still living in rebellion and ignorance. But God did answer those prayers. Though abandoned by the boy's father, Susan persevered in teaching her son, and eventually she came into contact with an Anglo-Saxon missionary couple with a deaf daughter. This family gave Susan a Bible and a lot of love. Then a total stranger sat down next to her on a train one day and said, "God has told me that there is someone in this train that I should speak to, and I believe that person is you." Susan was beautifully drawn back to the Savior she had sung about when she was eight. So, dear parent, don't give up hope. Even if you go to be with the Lord before your children turn back to Him, He will keep tracking them down with His love.

If your adult children are faithful and true to God, tell them how much that means to you. If there is a blockage, a breach or a barrier, I beg you to tear it down. In the name of Jesus, tell your children how much you love them. If you made mistakes, confess them to your children. Call them, write them, send an e-mail or a fax with one message — "I love you and I want us to be close for whatever time we have left."

If your children are still at home, close this book and go to them. Touch them. Tell them how proud you are to be their parent. Cherish them. Let them know how much you appreciate their response to Jesus. Tell them how important they are to you.

Your children don't always realize just how many advantages there are to being raised in a pastor's home. When the moment is right, be sure to remind them of all those perks. They have the extended family of the church as their family. They have built-in friends when they go to a new place. They are often the subject of the prayers of many godly people who realize that they may come under spiritual attack. They learn so much about the Bible and have a keen sense of what pleases God. They are taught to see everything from a Kingdom perspective and are not often fooled by the thin and empty things of life. Of course, you need to be realistic with them in admitting that their friends have other advantages.

If I had it to do over again, I would talk less about loving my family and I would put my love in action more often. Every week

without fail I would share a quality event with my boys. I would
have a date night with my wife every week without fail. I would
honor my family by taking a day off every week. I would not burden them with the challenges I faced at church, but I would let
them know just how valuable they are to me.

We have found in the pastoral ministries department at
Focus on the Family that the primary impediments to a healthy
ministry family are not church politics or even economic disad-
vantages. The problems for children stem from a lack of loving
deeds and from poor communication between the ministry couple and the children.

Let me ask two searching questions: Does your family know
without a doubt that they are the most important thing in your
life? And do they know you love them more than anything? I
pray so.

Let me share suggestions for communicating love to your
family:

*Let children be children.*
Kids are not miniature saints or small adults. Church
members should not expect more from your children
than they do from their own. Play down the common
notion that they are to be examples. Emphasize the ideal
that every believer has the privilege of being as much like
Christ as possible. All Christian children are expected to
love Christ, and this expectation is not placed on them
so much by their parents as it is by Christ Himself. And
Christ specializes in loving the weakest and the most
needy among us.

*Teach your children to respect others and holy places.*
If you have draining individuals in your church, take

care to keep the frustrations you feel about these persons from your children. Teach your children to look up to mature believers. Also encourage your children to have respect for the sanctuary, the altar, the pulpit, the musical instruments and the communion table.

*Don't forget to shepherd your own children.*
Talk to them early about God, so you can keep on talking to them about the Father when they are older. Try making faith development in your home as natural as the air you breathe. The children who live at your house are as important to God as anyone on the face of the earth. You are the only pastor they may ever have.

*Connect parenting and pastoring skills.*
As you practice and polish these skills, think about the many positive ways pastoring is like parenting. Like parenting, pastoring involves encouragement, direction and sometimes correction. Also, think of joy, contentment, fulfillment and pride. Consider the wonderful satisfaction parents receive from doing their work well. Similar satisfactions come from effective pastoring.

*Love your children to greatness.*
Christians are never nagged into becoming something important for God. Stalwart believers are shaped by models, mentors and a wise word spoken at a time of need or blessing. Stay open to learn new ways of showing your children love. Turn your affection into a series of actions that convinces your church that your children are significant to you, that they are the most important people in your life.

Neil tells about an insightful conversation with a great Christian leader who had been retired for several years. With insight gained from many years of faithful ministry, the leader remarked, "When the sun starts to set, the only thing left is God and your family."

—H. B. L.

# give yourself
# a great marriage

Denominational headquarters may seem like a strange place for a couple to meet, but that's the way it happened for us. It started with a bit of subtle flirting in the lunchroom. We were both 24 and had finished college. We mistakenly thought we were so ancient that we were doomed to singleness. In our day, most young people our age were already married or were at least engaged. Bonnie was executive secretary to top leaders in our church—she knew a lot and said little about the inner workings of the denomination. I was a seminary student, doing part-time editorial work in the Christian education section. Bonnie came from two generations of preachers, and I was raised by young parents who ultimately were related for 50 years to the little church in Detroit, where I grew up. By the time we met, she had moved 11 times and I had moved only twice.

She knew a lot about ministry from her years in a parsonage, and I had experienced only one church. It was in the 1950s, and times were good. I had the call to be a pastor. We married the next year, and I took a student pastorate within two months of our wedding. Since then we have had a few hard times, but mostly good. And we have been in continuous pastoral or teaching ministry ever since then. As the poet said, the years teach.

Soon after we started dating, she let me know in a quiet way that she did not plan to marry a pastor. Though marriage was not in my immediate plans, I began to realize that should we become a couple, Bonnie would not be marrying a pastor, so much as she would be marrying *me*, who just happened to be a pastor. That one idea has saved us from being bound by ministry stereotypes and old wives' tales about preachers. The union of a man and a woman is an expression of their love for each other and of their desire to spend their life together. As John Lubbock said in 1909, "Adam could not be happy even in Paradise without Eve."[1]

Focusing on creating a life together is much more satisfying and fun than placing a marriage/ministry expectation template over your relationship. It is off track to assume that a clergy marriage will experience greater difficulties than any other—or fewer, for that matter.

Let Bonnie and me share several ways that ministry couples can give themselves the gift of a stronger and more satisfying marriage:

*Communicate.*
Speak up in your marriage relationship, so it is clear what each of you needs and wants. Take a long walk and talk about ways to strengthen your marriage. Get away from interruptions, talk candidly and renew the passion of your youth. Tell each other what is just as important today as when you started. Talk about your dreams, your fears and your souls.

*Speak up to the children.*
Help them know your love for each other is the strong glue that holds everything together in your family. Model a strong marriage so your children develop into good marriage partners by what they see in you.

*Speak up to the church.*
Help your church people understand a pastor serves bet-

ter when relationships are going well at home. Let them know you want to build and maintain a strong marriage and family for yourself and for the sake of your ministry to them. Reasonable people will honor and appreciate that priority.

Keep talking with your spouse until you come to mutual understanding, but keep in mind that marriage always possesses some degree of mystery between a man and a woman. That fact makes marriage intriguing and interesting and brings pleasant surprises across the years.

*Fulfillment produces contentment.*
Both your ministry and your marriage will flourish when you feel unconditional love from your spouse. Being married to a contented person is more fun than constantly dragging a partner out of the swamp of frustration and despair. Marriage success spills over into other areas of life. The opposite is also true. Don't ever forget that a faltering marriage wrings all satisfaction out of ministry; it cripples husband and wife emotionally and affects everything they do or say, whether to church members, family or neighbors.

*Cherish the cause you love.*
You should never serve in a place where you are not challenged. Our Lord has given the Church an important mission in the world, and implementing that mission is the way pastors find meaning and fulfillment. When you are committed to a great cause, you will not be haunted by the age-old question, "Does my life count for anything?" Many pastors do not have meaning in their lives

because they do not see their work as part of the great work God is doing in the world. Love your church to greatness. As a couple, share your dreams and commitments to Christ and His Church.

*Recognize you are an original.*
Husband and wife have been uniquely created by God. This means every pastor and spouse do their work differently from anyone else in the universe. Therefore, since God created every person different and every church unique, it follows that every pastor has a specific work to do in a particular assignment that no one has ever done before in that place. To make the marriage special, each ministry couple must realize and cherish the unique and special ability given each of them by God. Cherish the liberty the Lord allows us in methodology and marvel over how He assigns us so often to places where we especially fit.

*Keep the gender war outside your relationship.*
The so-called battle between the sexes in society has allowed cynical attitudes and caustic talk into too many parsonages and churches. For clergy couples to be happily married, these hostile attitudes must be kept out of their relationship. The most important issue is for each couple to build their own great marriage—not in the neighborhood, not in the community, not in the universe, but in their home. Working to enrich each other's lives and to give selfless, loving expressions of affirmation to each other are among a ministry couple's most important goals and most satisfying accomplishments. Since we live on earth as well as in the Kingdom realm,

we must not allow secular perspectives and values to affect our marriage.

*Commit to holy wholeness.*
Since all of us live in a dysfunctional society, we tend to believe that difficulties from our past are inevitable obstacles or a constant deadweight we have to carry. While the past cannot be changed, the good news of the gospel is that the spirit of Jesus can make us new. We can ask God to unchain us from past enslavements. The Christ-saturated life is available to all who earnestly seek holy wholeness.

Marriage almost inevitably faces serious trouble if either partner clings to unresolved problems from the past. We must individually find resolution to such problems and experience cleansing so that we can pour ourselves into our marriage relationship. Then, our happy, well-adjusted marriages can be convincing expressions of ministry to the flock of God and to those outside the Church.

*Strive for family solidarity.*
We all know families in constant crisis. Do they find trouble, or does trouble follow them? When crises strike again and again in a minister's home, both the pastor and the family are handicapped in their service to others. Naturally, if they feel so paralyzed that they can no longer minister for Christ, they feel miserable. Should this be the case in your home, you must ask yourself honestly if there is some pattern of destructive behavior at the root of such crises. The inability to control a bad attitude, an imbalance in time use or poor financial choices are exam-

ples of a few culprits. If your conduct causes your crises, change it. Husbands and wives must listen carefully to each other in order to overcome such weaknesses.

However, God sometimes allows many crises into the lives of those who are extremely faithful. One only has to remember the trials of poor Joseph in Egypt. When bad things happen to the minister's family, we must not jump to conclusions. Jesus taught us to expect persecutions and sufferings. The challenge is to make sure the emotional and spiritual tone of our families is not entirely dictated by outside forces, whether they be the local congregation, the community or anyone else. We must resist the impact of those external influences and keep our wills set to do the will of God. Though you may not wish to think about it, your years at home with your children slip away quickly as they grow and develop. Make the most of your opportunities with them. While your family may never be perfect, strive to improve it in every way possible.

*Seek solutions and satisfaction.*
Some pastoral assignments are filled with land mines waiting to explode in the minister's marriage. Nonetheless, complaining about hardship leads nowhere. Why not face the fears and tackle the obstacles? Many marriage aggravations are due to general human problems and are not distinct ministry issues. Who says you would not have struggled with exactly the same difficulties had you chosen to work in the computer field or in medicine?

If you want to take a giant step forward, you must gulp, take a big breath and look objectively at your marriage to identify difficulties and possibilities. Then initiate a candid discussion with your spouse. Move from generalized feelings of marriage malaise to identifiable issues you and your spouse can talk through and resolve. Neither marriage nor ministry are problems to be solved; they are gifts to be received and enjoyed.

God gave you marriage for companionship, pleasure, procreation and long-term joy—be sure not to miss the delight and satisfaction He intended for you to experience. Perhaps it would help to write out the innumerable blessings that ministry offers to a marriage. After counting the privileges, you can honestly inspire your spouse, your children and yourself with this thought, "Thank God for the unique and wonderful benefits He has given us in the privilege of being a married ministry couple."

—N. B. W.

## Note

1. Rebecca Davis and Susan Mesner, eds., *The Treasury of Religious and Spiritual Quotations* (Pleasantville, NY: Reader's Digest Association, 1994), p. 319.

# *in* Partnership

## with

## the

## fATHER

SECTION 5

# dare to dream great dreams

Someone I met on a trip to Australia defined insanity as: "Doing things the same way while expecting different results."

What an accurate description of so many churches. We do the same things over and over, expecting that our results will suddenly be different or improved. If we refuse to change methods and fail to serve Christ in better ways, we will get the same results we are getting now.

In the United States, a lower percentage of people claim Christianity as their faith now than they did 10 years ago. And the downward trend continues. If we can't stop this slide, the Church will be significantly weaker next year and perhaps even more tepid a decade from now.

If the Church is to be turned around, pastors must dream God's dream for their situations. Now I love to dream, because dreams create the possibility of new outcomes. Dreams produce hope. A leader who has a dream is inspired by it both in perspective and in preaching. Dreams help a church realize they can be more than they ever thought they could be. And when implemented, dreams increase a church's ability to address the world's concerns.

By daring to dream great dreams, miracles are not guaranteed, but it sure does make it interesting. The Church is engaged in a spiritual effort, and the results depend on the powerful work of the Holy Spirit to change hearts. But it is because the Church is a partner with the life-giving Spirit that she can expect great things from God. As Paul put it, "That power is like the working of his mighty strength, which he exerted in Christ when he raised him from the dead" Eph. 1:19,20). Pastor, because Christ lives and has authority over all things for the church, you can never outdream God, "who is able to do immeasurably more than all we ask or imagine, according to his power that is at work within us" (Eph. 3:20).

So, wherever I have opportunity to speak to laity, either privately or publicly, I urge them to allow their pastor to dream. I challenge them to help make those dreams come true. I push them to realize that dreams are where the future effectiveness of any church starts.

However, whenever I encourage the laity of a church to allow their pastor to dream, I go home worrying. What if they find out that their pastor has no dreams for the church? Let me be unmistakably clear—if a pastor doesn't dream and share those dreams with God's people, a church will succumb to the status quo, to apathy or to dry rot.

Dreams can be hindered by a pastor who will not dare to dream. They can also be hindered by members who refuse to follow the dream. Dreams may be a little scary, and somewhat dangerous. But we cannot spread the gospel of Jesus by marking time. The dreamer acknowledges the risks and then says, Follow me, as I follow Christ! Then, laying the church's plans before God and requesting His blessing and His indwelling Spirit, that pastor moves out, taking God's people along, to overcome obstacles in the powerful, risen name of Jesus Christ. Dream God's dream for your church. Talk about it everywhere you go.

Sometimes pastors must be ready for a lot of resistance. Let me illustrate. I attended a worship service in a great southern church. Arriving a little early, I took a seat on the aisle about halfway back. Before long, a spirited lady of about 70 stopped in the aisle and said, "Young man, are you going to sit in that place for the whole service?" I nodded that those were my plans. I looked about and saw there were many empty seats around us. She said to me, "Could you please sit somewhere else?" I asked her why. She replied, "I have been coming to this church for 15 years. Each Sunday I sit in the same place, and I doubt if I could worship if I sat anywhere else." Sitting two spaces over from me was not good enough. That's what I call being set in your ways.

Let me so be so bold as to say the Holy Spirit is the dream giver. He is the one who softens even the hardest heart to think positively about the dream. If you have any doubts, check out the book of Acts. The Spirit will assist pastors, staff members, lay leaders and congregations to find a path off the plateau, even if it is rocky at first. It is the Spirit's privilege and occupation to deepen unity within the Body of Christ. He stands ready to help us embrace a biblical pattern for the Church. The Spirit of God can touch even the hearts of the unresponsive.

I have sometimes joked with pastors, suggesting that if they want a new church, they have only to do one simple thing the next Sunday morning after the second song. Ask all the people from the right side if they would kindly move to the left side and have those on the left move right. Then they will have a new church. Some have actually tried it with success. Two things happen: You have the impression of speaking to a different congregation; and everyone in the pews now sees the church from a new perspective.

Remember, pastor—the dream never dies, only the dreamer; the song never stops, only the singer. Keep on dreaming. Keep on singing. Keep on believing with a holy audacity that God is doing a revolutionary work in your church. He wants to work through you to accomplish miraculous and eternal transformations where you serve. But, you ask, how?

*Try to understand what causes apathy.*

After you discover what causes apathy, try to eliminate it. The lay-ministry revolution and the secular volunteer movement taking place in the country have created greater willingness to volunteer at church. Apathy dissolves when people see a worthy reason for participation and when they receive spiritual satisfaction from serving. People are also more eager to become involved when they see that their service makes a difference. The laity want to share ministry and receive some of the same warm satisfaction for doing it well that pastors often enjoy. Get your people to pray concerning the apathy issue. And as they pray, the Holy Spirit will direct them to more useful service for the Kingdom.

*Dream God's dream for your assignment.*

Start by reading Acts 2 again and see what it says about visions and dreams. The Bible is filled with stories of people who sought the face of God for His will in their situation. After they discovered His will, they went to work to make it a reality. Some faced great hindrances and obstacles, and some even laid down their lives for the sake of the gospel. The risks are there, but when we remember Who gave the dream and what He has promised us, they are not so very frightening after all.

*Don't bleed for silly change.*

We've discussed change from several angles already, but some visionary leaders, in an attempt to move the church forward, can become confused about true progress and change for the sake of change. If your new ideas will not produce better results than the programs and ministries already in place, why suffer for them? Find and implement changes that make a difference. One church war started over which room a Sunday School class would use each Sunday; everyone chose up sides. Another church split over a change in the starting time on Sunday morning. How silly. Keep out of unproductive controversies. On the contrary, take a stand and bravely walk into controversies that will make your church more effective. Be sure to know the difference.

*Find ways to win people.*

New converts are a great source of inspiration for churches that have run aground. They remember where they were only a few months earlier. They have just witnessed the miraculous power of God's grace. Don't rant about apathy, but rather, win new people to defeat it.

*Team up with God.*

Check Scripture, and fast and pray until you find God's direction for your church. Be prepared for the strong probability that His purpose may not sound like what you heard at the last pastors' seminar. Wait before God until you have a vision of what can be done in your assignment. Ask others to seek God with you. Saturate your plans with Scripture. He has a doable plan for every place. Is anything impossible for God? (See Luke 1:37.)

"We've dreamed many dreams that never came true. We've seen them vanish at dawn. But we've realized enough of our dreams, thank God, to make us want to dream on!"[1]

—H. B. L.

**Note**
1. H. B. London, Jr., and Neil B. Wiseman, *The Heart of a Great Pastor* (Ventura, CA: Regal Books, 1994), p. 250.

# the pursuit of personal holiness

Personal holiness stands at the core of any pastor's ministry. Its potential, availability and promise are among my most fulfilling discoveries. Bob Jackson's song "The Upper Room" communicates a compelling message I recommend to every pastor. The basic thought is that if we leave behind all the busyness that distracts and find our upper room, we will be baptized with power from on high.

When I stood in the original Upper Room near Jerusalem, Jackson's song took on special meaning. Although no one can be sure the site is the exact biblical place, I could still imagine what it must have been like to be among the 120 waiting together in the Upper Room for the promised Holy Spirit. Something miraculous changed a motley, ordinary, doubting group of frightened followers of Jesus into a force that shaped the world. Pentecost was a defining moment. I'm sure those who were there freeze-framed the experience forever in their memories. It was a miraculous milestone—a unique event that turned the world upside down.

It is obvious from the New Testament story that the disciples' hunger for personal piety and their vision for worldwide evangelization started in the Upper Room. The experience they had there so marked and shaped them that they could never get over its effects. But, of course, they never wanted to get away from the piety and the passion they received there; piety born of the power of the Spirit, passion born of the love for Christ that He infused in their souls that day.

I once had my own upper-room experience. I really needed it, and I have never been the same since. I had come to the end of myself, and there I found a new power for ministry from God.

I was a successful young pastor—at least in the eyes of the Church and of the world. In fact, I was quite successful in my own eyes, as well. Glad to be noticed, I thought I rather deserved the success I was experiencing. It was a case of too much too soon. As the months went by, my ego grew even more inflated as others recognized me. I flew from conference to conference around the country telling others how to do ministry. At that time I was serving a congregation with a great history and an outstanding tradition. Attendance was growing, membership was increasing and we couldn't explain how it was all happening. But secretly I thought my own gifts had a lot to do with it, and I enjoyed telling others how to do God's work.

One Saturday afternoon, having returned from a tell-the-success-story trip, I was sitting at my desk in the church study. I wasn't ready for Sunday. I had not been praying. I had not been reading my Bible. I was running on my own adrenaline, just barely getting by. Suddenly I could see myself for what I was—a phony. I saw how out of sync I was with the Lord. I felt a desperation to find my place in His vineyard—not one of my making, but one made by Him for me.

Considering what I was experiencing, I had to have help. It was dusk when I called Beverley and said, "Honey, I will not be home for a while. I'll be there when I can get there, but don't worry. I have something important to do."

Then I went into the sanctuary. Our church in Salem, Oregon, had a beautiful worship center with a huge stained glass window that caught the last glimmers of daylight. I remember walking down that center aisle of the sanctuary as orange, red and blue hues dimly cascaded off the carpet. I literally laid myself prostrate at the altar in front of the pulpit and began to cry like a baby. I told the Lord, "I feel so crummy. I feel so dirty. I feel so unclean. I feel so unwholesome. And Lord, you must think the same about me."

Then with agony of spirit I continued, "Lord, why have You allowed me this success when You know the condition of my soul? Why have You brought me to this place of ministry when You know what I am on the inside? Why am I confused and frustrated when I should have so much joy in my work?"

Then I began to bargain with God: "Father, if we could just get me out of this situation without embarrassing me or You or this church, I'd gladly move away. Just let someone else come in and pastor this place."

I am not sure whether the Lord actually spoke to me or if I was just impressed in my spirit. But in that quiet moment I heard from God, and I knew it. His message was clear, "H. B., if you are really serious about what you have been praying, then I can use you. We can work together. Are you really serious?"

In those moments, I tore up the contract I had made years before with God. Now I simply said, "Father, here's a blank sheet of paper with my name signed at the bottom. You fill in the blanks. You write instructions. You give directions. In this moment of full surrender, I give You all I have to give. I'm totally Yours, now and forever. I'm tired of things as they are now." Since that day I have never been the same.

Three things happened almost instantaneously as a result of that encounter. First, the Word of God began to appear to me in a way I had never known it before. Its message leaped off the pages and touched my heart and then my lips. The second thing was that I began to love people genuinely and unconditionally. I no longer saw them as parishioners or customers for the church. Suddenly, they were individuals for whom Jesus died, and my heart felt broken by the things that break the heart of Jesus. And the third thing, I began to speak the Word of God with boldness. I experienced an anointing in preaching and courage for leadership I had never known before.

In an instant, I saw all my head knowledge, book knowledge and heart knowledge as nothing. There was only God. No skill, no ability, no experience, no insight is worth anything without the Lord's presence. It was a moment when this insecure, ego-driven, lonely, only child from the Midwest was touched by God. I realized I had been given an opportunity to do something incredibly important for Him in the church I served.

As a follow-up on that experience, I continue to look into the face of God and ask, "Am I OK? Is it well with my soul? Are you happy, Lord, with what you see? Search my mind. Search my thoughts. Search my attitudes. Please tell me if there is something about me that needs to be changed, because I don't want to be a stumbling block to anyone. Nor do I want to embarrass You." And He answers those prayers, sometimes—many times—with painful correctives, but always as a loving Father.

I beg every pastor reading this book to be honest with yourself about your inner life. Tattle to God on yourself. Is there something inside you that is stuck on how much you have accomplished? How much you know? How good your record is? He will not be surprised.

Let me remind you again that without God we can do nothing, and without us, God will not work. It is His mysterious design to use His ministers to announce His Word and to show Himself to the world. The path to a victorious ministry is paved with commitment, humility and authenticity, as well as competence. Every skill you possess for ministry is useful to God only when it flows from a pure heart.

What are some practical ways to implement these ideas about personal holiness?

*Work diligently at personal spiritual formation.*

The spiritual development of a pastor is no more automatic than it is for anyone else. It must be intentional and planned. Three short prayers keep ministry focused: Search me, break me, and use me. Find your method for developing personal holiness and work at it. Abundant reserves are available, but they have no effect until they are used.

*Take inner issues to the Lord.*

Some pastors are too proud and others too given to feelings of inferiority. Perhaps every human being, especially Christian workers, has some inner issue that needs the light of God to illuminate and heal. Some stew continually over some dark inner poison of which they are ashamed. Ask God to help you face your issues. Then seek His counsel about how to get victory so you can serve God as a whole person. Ultimately, both pride and false humility are stumbling blocks to genuine piety.

*Commit to your church's uniqueness.*

The church is essentially different from every other organization. In our time, well-intentioned Christians have worked hard to understand and use secular management strategies and principles in churches. Of course, churches can sometimes use such principles effectively, perhaps because some of them are borrowed from the biblical record. But keep reminding yourself that the church is significantly different at its heart from a business. Businesses sell products and receive profits. Churches give away the infinite treasure of the gospel. The goal of the church is to follow Christ, whatever the cost, in order to win souls, to help them find true life in

Jesus, and to prepare them for heaven.

I strongly recommend that we get back to the question, "How does God want us to operate this church at this time in its history?"

*Take your dryness and emptiness to the Lord.*
Spiritual resources tend to get used up as we work with congregations and their problems. As a result, spiritual resources must be renewed frequently or the pastoral leader becomes weak, lame and shallow. If you are living in a state of spiritual scarcity, pray for a heavenly deluge to fill up your emptiness and water your dryness.

*Give careful attention to basics.*
Put prayer, Bible reading and listening to God back into the fundamental commitments of your ministry and at the center of your church's efforts. The wrappings and delivery systems of ministry can and should change with each new generation. But no church in any generation can be a church without prayer, Bible reading and listening to God. Styles of soul winning, worshiping, preaching, singing, caring for members, discipling new believers and running the offices may change, but the spiritual basics must undergird it all, if a church is to weather the storms of controversy that it faces continually in this society.

Your personal holiness is of critical importance to the effectiveness of your ministry and the accomplishments of your church.

—H. B. L.

# CHRISTLIKENESS— a marvelous magnetism

"What first attracted you to church?" is a great conversation starter when you meet another Christian. For those born into Christian families, the question might better be asked of parents or grandparents. But whoever first came to church, came because of Christ. Jesus boldly announced that He would draw all people to Himself when He is lifted up. And He does.

Christ attracts. He draws people to himself and challenges them with His cause. The Lord Jesus is the magnificent magnet that draws us into His Church. But a spin-off question also needs to be considered.

A convert in a new church raised the second query when I asked, "What attracted you to the church?" My new friend replied, "You should also ask, 'Why did I keep coming?' " Then he came to the heart of the matter: "Christlikeness answers both questions. I saw Jesus in people in this church. That is why I came the first time, and that is why I keep coming." He is right—Christlikeness attracts people and Christlikeness keeps them coming.

Christ and His likeness developing in us make churches healthy and help them grow. Christlikeness attracts people to the Savior. Meanwhile, Christlikeness continually changes Christians into the image of our Lord—that's quality growth.

Let's try to scratch the surface of how Christlikeness builds and strengthens churches:

*Christlikeness provides meaning.*
Searching people discover meaning when they see Christlike characteristics such as love, forgiveness, grace, compassion and caring lived out in the church. Deep within, everybody wants and needs everything on that list, and that is what Jesus intends His Church to offer on His behalf. Genuine Christlikeness helps persons find meaning, fulfillment and purpose.

*Christlikeness requires spiritual stretching.*
Being molded into Christlikeness forces the people of God to stretch to be what the Father wants them to be. Just as physical exercise conditions one's body, spiritual stretching strengthens one's soul. As a result, the witness and walk of God's people become more authentic. Their way of living becomes appealing and inspiring to others. And their Christian witness becomes more convincing.

*Christlikeness renews a congregation.*
The Body of Christ repairs itself as it draws near her Lord. As a healthy human body throws off infection and heals itself of a simple cut, Christlikeness helps a church protect itself against germs of secularism, viruses of doctrinal confusion and the crippling pain of troubled relationships.

Genuine renewal restores a church to health, so that it grows naturally. Any church, because it is a living cell of the universal Church, can experience renewal and restoration. But to enjoy robust health, a church must frequently measure its Christlikeness. Using what it discovers about itself, a congregation must make needed corrections in order to become the church God wants it to be. Even though the prescription may call for radical confession, extravagant generosity and all-out outreach, the results are well worth any price.

*Christlikeness makes a church attractive.*
A supernatural enthusiasm, fueled by miracles of grace, makes a church attractive to anyone seeking spiritual reality. This attractiveness is more than an emotional stir, an engaging musical beat, a raspy preacher or a charismatic-style service.

A church where Christ is to be seen will be empowered in everything it does by God's Spirit. Every phase of congregational life will be so saturated with Christlike behavior and attitudes that people who attend cannot wait to see what God is going to do next. In such a church, the atmosphere is so filled with holy love that members would rather be there than anywhere else.

In such a church, human trophies of God's grace surround us. Addicts are set free. Sinners are forgiven. Believers are filled with God's fullness. Marriages are healed. New pastors and missionaries are called into service. And society is led to the Redeemer by the redeemed.

*Christlikeness encourages self-criticism.*
Genuine Christlikeness compels those who lead a church to listen for an inner alarm when a church starts to veer off course. This closeness to Christ provides a built-in call to correction of mission, so the church sees

its work and its potential through the eyes of the Lord.

*Christlikeness connects us to an incredible cause.*
Christlikeness does not cost a person or a congregation much—just everything. Consequently, when willing to pay the price, every church regardless of size, setting, opportunity, constituency or budget can be like Christ. Every church can have His qualities of grace, His burden for the lost and His energy for ministry—what a combination.

Christlikeness makes any church an instrument of a magnificent cause—the work of God in the world. That connection to Christ makes even the most common congregation in the most remote outpost of the world a living part of the whole Church.

Let's weave authentic Christlikeness into the fabric of our churches, so His magnetism attracts people and keeps them coming Sunday by Sunday and year after year. Let's make Jesus the centerpiece of every phase of the church's ministry, and He will captivate us continually and draw many to Himself because of our ministry.

—N. B. W.

# a generous God honors extravagance

My passion for outreach missions started when Dr. Paul Smith spoke to our congregation. During his visit to our town, this pastor of the great, mission-minded People's Church in Toronto blessed us in the morning with a message based on 1 Corinthians 13. That afternoon before leaving, he addressed the Salem Academy High School graduating class at their baccalaureate service.

A few weeks later, Dr. Smith sent me a personal invitation to his church to observe their annual missionary conference. He did not ask me to speak but to soak up the inspiration of the conference. He bought my plane ticket, rented a car for me, provided lodging in a fine hotel and asked me to do nothing but to look and learn. And what a transformation took place in my mind.

I watched as his church of 3,000 people committed millions of dollars to overseas and home missions. They gave with such exuberance that it became contagious. That experience changed my ideas about my own church's potential to reach out with its money and man power to touch the whole world for Christ.

I returned to my congregation and said to anyone and everyone around me that we needed to do something above and beyond what we normally did. I shared my emerging dream: Let's build a church somewhere overseas. Let's raise money and send a team from our congregation to help with the construction. Our church members and friends responded with sacrificial generosity.

In accepting this challenge, they raised $25,000 over and above our normal missionary giving. That was a giant step in those days because we were already giving generously to world missions. Our plan was to set aside the extra $25,000 to build a church overseas.

That was in 1975. Until then, my denomination had had little experience with over-and-above missionary giving. So when I called our church headquarter's missions office to say the money was available, I asked, "Where would you like us to build a church?" Nobody seemed to know what to do with us. The permission process became complicated and confusing. Finally, I called again and said, "We have the money available, and we are going to build a church somewhere in the world. It doesn't have to be in our denomination. If you do not have a site for us to build a church, we will work through another missionary organization." That seemed to do the trick; I had an option of five locations in a short period of time.

We chose La Tinta, Guatemala, a remote place back in the interior near the Yucatan Peninsula. The church was to be built for the purpose of ministry to the Ketchi Indians, a little-known tribe who worked on coffee plantations and lived in poverty. The church was to be in honor of lifelong missionaries, Dr. and Mrs. William Sedat, who gave years of their lives translating the Bible into the Ketchi dialect. It took two years to build the church. When I was asked to return to dedicate the facility, it was filled with hundreds of people, and I was overjoyed. Because of the language barrier, I didn't understand much of that service; but I could rejoice in what our church had done. I celebrated the years of service given by the Sedats. I tried to imagine how many of the wonderful people in La Tinta would find Christ as a result of this new facility. Then, I especially thanked God for what this new mission thrust was doing for the spiritual vitality of our congregation. Subsequently, I thanked the Father for what He had allowed our church to do in this building project which, in turn, helped inspire the Work and Witness trips of hundreds of churches in North America.

Years later, after her husband's death and her retirement, I had the privilege of being Mrs. Sedat's pastor. It was a joy to listen as she told story after story of how God used that building we constructed in a remote area of Guatemala to win hundreds of Ketchi Indians. No one can possibly imagine the outcome of our generosity when blessed of the Lord.

Think of the small but powerful beginnings. It all started with a message and a friendly gesture by Dr. Paul Smith. Though Dr. Smith has since moved from Toronto to heaven, he taught me and my congregation that it's impossible to outgive God. He proved it in his life and in his great church. Dr. Smith understood that Christian generosity is motivated by the spendthrift God who gave His Son, Jesus Christ, for us. Christians respond to the challenge to give because of what Jesus gave for them.

The story goes on and multiplies beyond anything I could imagine. In the 1980s, we built a church in Korea. That congregation in Seoul caught our vision for building mission churches, so now they have built 15 churches in other parts of the world. And they will build more.

The lessons and benefits of generosity to God and others are hard to comprehend. I am still learning the lessons, and what I learn continues to amaze me. Pastor Eugene Peterson pushes and pulls me forward in greater generosity to God when he says:

> Some of us try desperately to hold on to ourselves, to live for ourselves. We look so bedraggled and pathetic doing it, hanging on to the dead branch of a bank account for dear life, afraid to risk ourselves on the untried wings of

giving. We don't think we can live generously because we have never tried. But the sooner we start the better, for we are going to have to give up our lives finally, and the longer we wait the less time we have for the soaring and swooping life of grace.[1]

But how can that challenge be lived out in your church?

*Value your influence.*
Dr. Paul Smith never knew the influence he had on my ministry and the outreach of the church I served. His weekend probably seemed routine for him. He traveled, as he had many a time, far from home to speak to a Christian high school. He preached on Sunday morning in my pulpit from a passage he had likely used many times before. He met and followed through on a new friendship with me. I, in turn, shared the vision with the congregation I served. They accepted the challenge and gave lots of new money. A church was built thousands of miles from our home. Other churches were built later. Every church we built now shares the gospel with neighbors and friends. Those who went overseas on missions trips to build churches increased their own generosity. The resulting influence continues and will grow forever.

*Test your suppositions.*
Under heavy financial pressure, a pastor may believe every dollar is needed in the local church. When you see the budget on paper and you consider the giving potential of your congregation, it is easy to become superconservative about overall stewardship and giving to causes outside the local congregation. But those reasoned

mathematical conclusions are human assumptions that ignore God's mysterious and miraculous math. God's math principles are these: If you hold on to what you have, you will have zero. If you give away what you have, in honor of Christ, you end up with infinite treasure. Try God's math in your church.

*Preach holy generosity.*
The idea is too outlandish for anyone else in the congregation to promote until they see it in action. If you want to lead a generous church, you will have to preach it, demonstrate it, talk about it everywhere and become partially consumed about the possibilities. The unselfish congregation and a generous pastor enjoy the benefits of this generosity. Notice, I did not suggest a say-it-and-claim-it approach. I simply believe God always outgives us and that we cannot be blessed with the results of generosity until we step out on faith and do something significant for God.

*Be a missionary.*
Allow the needs of the world to break your heart. Get close to those who give their lives to missions. Become prayer partners. Keep missionary information before your congregation. View yourself as a missionary to our pagan culture. Keep talking to your church about outreach, soul winning and witnessing at home and abroad. Visit mission fields, and share what breaks your heart with your congregation.

*Honor the spendthrift God.*
For years I have heard preachers say you can't outgive

God. Perhaps we can refocus that idea by measuring our giving against God's extravagant giving to us. Of course, we cannot in any ultimate sense give as He has given to us. But we can challenge our conservative views about giving, our fear of asking for money and our false conclusions that most people have given all they can give.

Call your people to hilarious generosity.

—H. B. L.

**Note**

1. Eugene Peterson, *Living the Message* (San Francisco: Harper, 1996), p. 124.

# keeping your sabbath holy

I enjoy visiting Israel for many reasons, but I especially like being there on their Sabbath. The bustle of life diminishes, and for 24 hours, the faithful do not go anywhere except to worship. They spend the Sabbath worshiping, talking, eating, and enjoying their families. Though they walk to the temple on Saturday morning, nearly everything else they do on the Sabbath happens at home.

Just thinking about the biblical concept of the Sabbath makes many ministers feel guilty because it is such a busy day for us. It seems an old-fashioned idea to many, yet for those who grew up in Christian homes, Sunday was a day of rest, and many Old Testament Sabbath principles were applied to the New Testament idea of respecting the Lord's day. In many homes, a special Sunday meal graced the dining-room table. Children were not to play outside, watch TV or do their homework. Some families would spend time reading the Bible together or would take part in services in nursing homes or hospitals. For others, the day was one for relaxation and time with the children. I know that there are many Christian views about Sabbath observance, and this book is not the place to lay them all out for discussion.

However, most Christians would agree that God instituted a day of rest for our good and for His glory. Some might argue that in the amazing presence of the Holy Spirit we actually give all seven days in service to our King Jesus. The apostle Paul does remind us that we are not to judge one another about holy days and Sabbaths. However, we can admit that we need physical reminders of God's great truths. Ever since the Resurrection, the Christian Church has met not on the seventh, but on the first day of each week, to celebrate our new life in Christ, to worship God, to refresh our souls by hearing His Word, and to bring our offerings to Him.

Pastors have a hard time with Sundays, however. Though we are certainly refreshed by serving our Lord, we are also exhausted. Most of our week's work comes to a head on weekends, and we can find ourselves running around frantically without remembering that God has asked us to spend a day resting. We excuse ourselves by rationalizing that we put the Kingdom first. However, when we refuse God's provision for us, we reap the effects in our family, church, personal stability and inner yearnings for Christlikeness.

In my early years as a pastor, I paid no attention to God's design in this area. When I arrived in Oregon, the church had just moved into a new building on which they had not made their first mortgage payment. There was space for the church to grow, I was filled with dreams and high energy, and the leaders accepted my ideas. I threw myself into the ministry, maybe trying to prove my worthiness to God—I'm sure I don't understand all the reasons.

I know now how foolish I was. I worked seven days a week, as many hours each day as it took. I seldom took a day off, and I was proud of my busyness obsession. I sent my family on vacations, met them for two or three days during the week and then flew home for the weekend. I gave lots of attention to winning men; I even used athletics as a means to be with men whom I tried to win to Christ. God blessed the church, and I thought everything was progressing wonderfully well. The church was doing well, but I wasn't.

Things fell apart one Sunday night as I was introducing a guest speaker. Suddenly I had no idea where I was. I was helped to my seat. Before long, someone came to the platform, guided me from the sanctuary, and took me home. For five weeks I didn't get out of bed. I had a virus and a nervous reaction brought on by exhaustion. Today my condition might be called incapacitating burnout.

My problem started where burnout always starts. I worked with the mistaken notion that I had to change the world by myself and do it quickly. I thought if I didn't change my world, nobody would. Thus, there were never enough hours in the day or days in the week to get ministry done. So I kept burning the candle at both ends.

I lost almost 30 pounds during my illness. My legs cramped so that I found it difficult to walk. I experienced deathly nausea every morning. Doctors came every day, gave me medication and cared for me. All this was five weeks from hell, during which I wondered if I would ever preach again. But that painful experience became a pivotal point for me when I started to see ministry, priorities and family relationships in new ways.

Of course, my misguided feelings seemed noble, but they were irresponsible and foolish. I remember what Beverley sometimes said after I commented from the pulpit, "I've not had a day off in four weeks." Or I sometimes said on Sunday morning, "I've been out most of the night ministering to someone in great need." Then she would say, "H. B., you are not impressing the congregation. They probably think you're crazy. They would rather have a pastor who is balanced than driven. Please don't say that silly stuff anymore."

After my health crisis started to improve, Bev and I had some serious conversations. "This can't happen again," we each said in our own way. We knew our family couldn't take it again, I couldn't take it again, and the church should not be expected to take it again.

As a type A personality, I had a terrible time changing my approach to ministry. I like to work. I love what I do. The crisis had taught me, however, that I should never again get so lost in ministry that I lose balance. You can understand that when I plead with you to find balance, I am not speaking from empty, bookish theory. I beg you to slow down so that you, your family and your congregation will not have to live through my experience, or maybe one much worse.

However you understand the Sabbath principle from the Scriptures, be sure to work its meaning into your life. Take weekly time away. Take time to be alone. Take time for God. Take time to get acquainted with yourself. Take time to be with your spouse and family. Take time to shut the doors of the world for a while to give attention to your health and wellbeing. Solitude and service must be balanced in ministry—one without the other leads to emotional and spiritual bankruptcy.

I beg you to heed my message. If you are not taking care of yourself, please start now. Make a plan and live by it. If you are not taking time to be alone with God, make time as you would to be with your best friend. He is your most faithful mentor and your beloved Chief. By the way, when was the last time you had a physical?

Of course, keeping the Sabbath for you will be different than it is for your parishioners because of your heavy Sunday responsibilities. But you must find ways to make the benefits of the Sabbath a reality for you on another day. Check Scripture for the meaning and purpose of the Sabbath. In the Bible, the Sabbath was a time for refreshment, a time for practicing family religion, a time for reflection, a time to reexamine priorities and a time of quiet solitude with God. We all have gauges inside us like the instruments on the dashboards of our automobiles. When your gauge marked "spiritual," "emotional," "physical" or "family" sits on empty or even at the half-full mark, you must take action and do it quickly. You can improve the benefits of your personal Sabbath by considering these possibilities:

*Practice contentment.*

Too many ministers are in a continual frenzy about what comes next. Serve with all your might where you are. Do your work so well that you will be happy with the results if you stay in your present assignment for the rest of your life. Consider Paul's statement and its implications in your life, "Godliness with contentment is great gain" (1 Tim. 6:6).

*Associate with balanced people.*

Friends feed off one another's perspective of life. If you spend time with people who are out of balance, you may start to tilt a little yourself. On the contrary, if you associate with believers who make room for what matters without going crazy, you will find yourself walking along the balance beam of life with a little more confidence. Though I can't explain it fully, I believe a commitment to balance is contagious.

*Remember energy cannot be hoarded.*

Energy cannot be saved like money in the bank. You must use your energy for what really matters, rather than wasting it on nonessentials. Though energy cannot be stockpiled, it can be invested in ministries that last for eternity.

*Find a level of ministry somewhere between boredom and frenzy.*
Some ministry tasks are so routine you can do them without much thought or planning. Learn to do them well and then move on to something more challenging. Give your passion to the big stuff and learn to do the routine stuff without panic.

*Try asking God to approve your schedule.*
At the start of your day, discuss the time demands of that day with the Father. Ask Him to direct, enable and use you. Sometimes after we consult the Father, what we consider to be essential gets pushed down the scale of significance.

*Continually upgrade your way of doing things.*
Sermon preparation should take a different amount of time in the first decade than in the fourth decade of your ministry. Keep asking yourself how modern technology can increase your effectiveness. At the same time, over-rule any tendency to become a technology nerd.

*Do things right the first time.*
The idea came from a quality program instituted by Johnson and Johnson during the 1980s. The secret is to go for small wins and improve everything you do in some way. A constant accumulation of improvement soon grows into a ministry of excellence.

*Treat church members like partners.*
Partners take part in the firm's effort. They are not merely to be served, but are to serve others. Too many church members suffer because the minister either expects too

much of them or not enough. If you invest energy in training your partners and your members, you will save yourself enough time to enjoy one day off each week. Someone else may need to serve Christ by doing what you have jealously guarded for yourself. So give the job over, and let Christ do it with someone else's arms and legs. How you decide to deal with these issues will have a huge bearing on how you use your time and whether you take the time to enjoy God's day of rest.

—H. B. L.

# are you sure you want what you think you want?

The sovereignty of God is easy to overlook in the details of church life. I forgot about it once in a time of great pastoral prosperity and achievement.

The congregation was growing by leaps and bounds. Our progress seemed blessed by the Lord. We added facilities— Sunday School rooms, sanctuary additions and parking lots. Soon we decided we should buy some adjacent property where we could construct new facilities.

No one had anticipated how ferociously our neighbors would oppose such a project. They fought us all the way to the Oregon State Supreme Court. We pushed and pulled to get our way—from the planning commission to the city council—until finally our case was heard by the highest state court. We worked hard to understand our rights, and we exercised them with gusto. By the time our case came up, we had spent thousands and thousands of dollars securing the services of the finest attorneys in our community.

At the same time, we kept working toward our new building. We planned, talked and even prayed. All this was taking place in the early 1980s when interest rates started to climb. As our case moved slowly up the judicial ladder, the rates climbed quickly to staggering heights. Soon our projected monthly payments began to give us sleepless nights. The long march through the endless maze of governmental bureaucracy was a tedious process that my energetic personality found hard to accept. We seemed to take two steps back for every three steps forward.

Finally, the Oregon State Supreme Court overruled earlier judgments, and we were granted approval to have our area zoned for a new church building. On the surface we had won. But interest rates had gone so high by that time that had we borrowed money to build, we would have compromised the congregation's very existence. Our debt would have been so massive that we would have been plunged into financial ruin. As I think back on those difficult days, I realize that God allowed us our desire, while knowing from the beginning we would not be able to build that building.

There is an interesting postscript to this story. After I left the church, the congregation was afraid that they could not afford to build where they were, and they purchased property for possible relocation. Some thought, even then, that the new property would never be the right place for a church. A short time ago, that property was sold for a profit of nearly 1 million dollars. Rather than spend all that money on themselves, they gave 20 percent of it to mission groups, Christian colleges and parachurch organizations.

The latest decision is to stay put. They plan to refurbish, make maximum use of facilities and keep all ministries so attractive that others will want to attend in spite of crowded conditions. They can do that and do it well.

A lesson for pastors comes from our experiences: God rules and overrules in His Church. Everything we think we need may not be His will. God keeps patient with us because He sees the end from the beginning. I'm sure you know what I'm talking about. There are probably many situations in your own life that testify to God's wisdom and to your misunderstanding of His will. He cares for us, and His solutions arrive on time. I have learned the hard way that God sometimes gives us what we want but hinders us from getting what we expect. Let's think about ways to be sure we are in sync with the Master Leader:

*Welcome God into the details.*
We find it easier to trust God for the big things, which we can't control anyway, than we do for the small things that seem to be within our grasp. Order your ministry by the principle that you will always seek the divine will in everything you do. When our desires are motivated by our love for Christ, and for our brothers and sisters in the congregation, He will direct us through the everyday, sensible decisions we are called to make so often. Don't be fooled into thinking that if you don't feel some tingling in your heart, it can't be the will of God. When you are not certain what path to take, you can always, as Elisabeth Elliot puts it, "do the next thing." Do your best thinking and give your best commitment to finding the godly course of action.

Sometimes, of course, the best route is to stand still until you are sure. When everything seems tight and nothing seems to be moving, it is a good time to wait until the Father's plan becomes crystal clear. God's waiting room can become a place to learn the satisfying experience of absolute dependence on Him.

*His timing is not always easy to understand.*
Hindsight helps us see that God is at work even when He is silent or slow by our standards. Like my friend Reuben Welch likes to say, "Even when nothing is happening, something is happening." One of the most encouraging

aspects of ministry is to know for sure that God is dependable. The promises of the nearby God are true and trustworthy.

### Don't push to get your way.

I am always a little frightened by what Scripture says about the children of Israel: "He gave them their request; but sent leanness into their soul" (Ps. 106:15, *KJV*). On the contrary, I find happy encouragement from Oswald Chambers: "Faith never knows where it is being led, but it knows and loves the One who is leading."[1]

### View administration as a part of God's grand scheme.

For three decades or more, church leaders have worked hard to learn skills from business leaders and social scientists for advancing the Church. Secular leadership literature has much to teach us—but not everything. If pastoral leadership really means partnership with God, then He is the pastor's best consultant, and His will is the best plan for His Church. Though it might make me sound like an old fogy, I believe decision groups at every level of the Church need more prayer meetings and fewer business seminars.

### Ask God for His perspective.

The church I served at Salem so many years ago is still using the same facilities and plans to do so for many years. Worldly wisdom said to build. But God had other plans. I am *not* suggesting that all building programs should be delayed or abandoned. I *am* suggesting that we open ourselves to new direction from our loving Father, who knows the past, present and future as if they were one. He will write the final chapter for all of us and for every church. And when it is written, His awards will go to those who have loved Him and trusted Him all along.

—H. B. L.

**Note**
1. Oswald Chambers, *Daily Thoughts for Disciples* (Fort Washington, PA: Christian Literature Crusade, 1976), p. 18.

# two more
# compelling legacies

My old preacher friend was greatly troubled as he lay dying. He wanted to be sure his life had really counted for God. He had served small churches all his life. He could not think of many miraculous experiences in his ministry. But 40 years of preaching, caring and serving made up an impressive accumulation. Before we were in his sickroom long, he shared a biblical passage that encouraged him many times: "We continually remember before our God and Father your work produced by faith, your labor prompted by love, and your endurance inspired by hope in our Lord Jesus Christ" (1 Thess. 1:3). What a joyful time we had as we assured him his ministry was exceedingly effective when measured against that passage.

As we sang and prayed and rejoiced around his hospital bed, we reminded him of the multiple legacies faithful pastors like him leave the rest of us.

Of course, love tops the list—it is amazing and magnificent and influences everyone, including unborn generations. A loving act often has a life of its own that continues beyond our ability to imagine. Today I remember gestures of love and kindness shown me more than 40 years ago.

Beyond love, or perhaps because of it, two more legacies endure. The first is the spiritual impact you, as pastor, make on those you lead. And the second is those who are called into God's service under your ministry.

Consider your spiritual influence. A pastor's greatest adventure is winning people to Christ and helping them develop in the faith. Pastors sometimes commit energy and imagination to building great institutions or impressive buildings, but the most essential contribution of a life of ministry is the great people of faith and devotion who emerge. Increasingly, newer literature for pastors focuses on building healthy churches rather than building great crowds. I love this emphasis which seems so new, though it is as old as the New Testament. The bottom line—healthy churches produce spiritually healthy believers.

Try taking an audit of spiritual influence that radiates from your life. What will people remember after you're gone? In the tiny church of my childhood, each pastor left us a special legacy.

Patience Hole, a woman pastor who had great faith, helped us believe God could do anything even in the smallest of groups, and He did.

Robert North, self-made minister, modeled hard work, perseverance and devotion to family; our congregation observed rich real-life dimensions of faith in him and from him.

Charles Hoos, one of God's busiest activists, demonstrated how faith without works is dead by remodeling the church with his own hands, caring for his four children as a single parent, gathering food and clothing for the destitute, and preaching to us as if we were the most important congregation God ever gave a preacher. We laughed in love as he worked with a hammer in one hand and a Bible in the other, and carried a homemade birthday cake for a church member on the back seat of his car.

Notice, these pastors are not remembered for brilliance or finely tuned administration skills, but for their life-changing impact on others.

Those who go into Christian service become another legacy leaders leave. Personal mentoring of a youth by the pastor may explain why Christian workers most often come from small, out-of-the-way churches. One-on-one care given in a small church's personalized ministry trains young people better than many more sophisticated programs. One 68-year-old retired pastor realized, when he took stock of his ministry, that he had mentored 20 pastors into ministry across his years of service. Who can count the eternal consequences of that magnificent record? Only in heaven will that dear child of God get to see the fruitful and joyful results of his faithful love to 20 young Christians. Pastors have a high privilege to be able to influence these young leaders. Please, pastors, if you have the chance to work with interns or trainees, don't turn a cold shoulder to them. Of course they will not know how to preach very well. Think of your first sermon and have mercy on them. Of course they will pull some blunders with the church's neat freak until they realize how to handle her. But stay patient. These young servants of Christ are some of the Church's most valuable assets for the future. Those called under your ministry are likely to preach and teach and influence lives long years after you are gone, and in places you could never go.

If you have spent any time in active ministry, you have probably had someone encourage you to listen to God's directive for your life. Now it is time to pass that same encouragement on to the next, and thus to the succeeding, generations. When ministers come to the twilight years of their service, they will rejoice to see that God has multiplied their ministry again and again. What a legacy that becomes, and what assurance it provides a pastor.

Accomplishments often have to do with bricks and buildings. Or with mission and message. Or with purpose and people. I know which of the six accomplishments I prefer. Though the variety of accomplishments is infinite, one question must always be asked in the secret place where our soul meets God: "Have I accomplished what God wants done here?"

This legacy of achievement is important to the pastor and of supreme importance to the Kingdom. Without new converts, maturing believers and a rejuvenating leadership, the Church has a limited future. A wall plaque in my childhood home clearly explains the main issue of legacy: "Only one life, 'twill soon be past; only what's done for Christ will last." And our Lord calls us to produce fruit that will remain.

Legacy—what a sobering challenge and what an incredible opportunity. How can we strengthen the possibility that our legacy will be pleasing to the Savior?

*Analyze your situation.*
Determine what is important for you to accomplish in your present assignment and do it. The task, persons and achievement will be different than they have been in any other setting.

*Create a climate of obedience.*
These days, persons of all ages are being called into various phases of Christian ministry. Preach about how fulfilling it is to follow the will of God. Rejoice in public that God chose you to be a minister. Ask your young people if they are listening for a call.

*Keep your perspective.*
Ask God to show you the difference between the temporary and the abiding. It is so easy to confuse the urgent with the important.

*Discuss legacy with mature believers.*
Though few may know how to describe lasting impact on them in terms of legacies, you can ask them what

they remember most about former pastors. Ask what mattered and why. Their response will assist you to map your ministry and audit your legacy.

*Remain accountable.*
Ask God to look you over. Check your motives. Keep thinking about the need to finish your earthly race of ministry well.

—N. B. W.

# maximizing your church's spiritual potential

Building and funding the new Denver International Airport created years of controversy in the media and in the councils of government. The debates continue, although the new airport has been open for years. However, even during the most heated debates, no one suggested altering the purpose of the project. Everyone agreed that they were out to improve the efficiency of the connection between the Rocky Mountain West and the rest of the world. Air travel is Denver International Airport's main business.

The airport's saga offers helpful parallels to contemporary ministry. Our essence—our reason for being—is to connect people with the living Christ. Sadly, churches sometimes neglect their main purpose, allowing themselves to become pleasant meeting places, holy clubs or religious shows. Perhaps the Church should reclaim her primary purpose and do what the Church does best. Adam and Eve's mandate was to cultivate the earth and to multiply. The Church's mandate is to do the same on a spiritual level. We must water and cultivate those under our care so that our churches bloom profusely and produce abundant fruit. I propose we give ourselves totally to our God-given mission and do it so well that we attract nonbelievers and nourish growth in the saints. Can we hear the thunder of the future? Can we make the main thing the main thing? Can we pour our energy, ingenuity and creativity into the spiritual potential of our churches? Of course, yes is our resounding answer. But how?

*Give your church the gift of Spirit-filled leaders.*
In evangelical circles, a pastor or lay leader is seldom asked about the condition of his or her soul. All those who preach, teach and lead must make the holy life personal. The leader must model a fulfilling lifestyle energized by a holy nearness with God.

*Build intentional intercession into the schedule.*
We all need others to pray more for us, and we need to pray for others. Selfless intercession is among the most powerful forces in the work of the gospel. Try increasing planned intercession in your church. Get your congregation to pray and the whole church will be lifted.

*Schedule renewal events into the annual program.*
No church can keep spiritually fit without regular seasons of refreshing renewal. Renewal must be deliberate. The secular world strangles spiritual stamina out of our people, so many of our parishioners feel spiritually spent and emotionally crippled. Renewal and refreshment get the weary Christian ready to return to the world.

*Make your administrative groups into a spiritual core group.*
Start implementing this concept in your next business meeting. Begin board meetings with prayer. Seek divine guidance before making pressing decisions. Use scriptural principles in solving problems among yourselves, and practice godly, humble leadership. What would hap-

pen to your business meetings if the first 20 minutes were taken in watering the souls of those gathered to help run the church? One pastor of a small church holds business meetings only quarterly. The other monthly meetings in the quarter are used for dreaming, planning and praying.

### Create meaningful encounters with Scripture.

Some of your members may still be thinking that the Bible is an antique book, full of rules and mysteries. Teach God's people that the Bible is a love letter from their heavenly Father. Speak about Scripture with clarity and affection. It needs less defense and more application to life.

### Refuel people when you preach.

Everyone loses when a pastor scolds, complains and reprimands. On the contrary, think how everyone grows when preaching generates courage, creates inspiration and challenges people to be overcomers. Feed them faith. Emphasize grace. Teach them to challenge and to pray through every hindrance.

### Celebrate victories.

Every church has many more victories than parishioners hear about. Sometimes we focus too much on problems. Sometimes we forget to praise God for answered prayer. Encourage people to share their victories and rejoice. Brag on the Lord's blessings. Soon faith will be stimulated and parishioners will begin expecting and receiving miracles. Many churches grow weary because there is little place in the church for such testimonies to God's triumph and grace. Perhaps you could open up a time of testimony in a smaller evening service or in a small group. Maybe you could choose a member—in whose life you know God has been at work—to come share what God has done. Maybe your church newsletter could concentrate a little less on times of meetings and names of committees and instead seek the stories of God's great grace that are going on among the people in your church. People are sometimes a little reluctant to share such things in public, but once they get used to it, they realize the excitement, enthusiasm and comfort they receive when they hear that God is indeed among them.

*Teach believers to live in the Presence.*
Centuries ago, the saintly Brother Lawrence discovered while doing monastery KP duty that a believer can find and enjoy the Presence as easily while washing greasy pots as at the Communion table. Think of the spiritual potential of teaching people to recognize God everywhere they go. I believe that is what Paul meant when he urged us to pray without ceasing and to give thanks in everything.

Your church's spiritual potential is a God-given resource, which you can easily cultivate. Without spiritual grit and truly godly hearts, God's people will only build with "wood and straw," as the apostle Paul says. But when Christians begin to think God's thoughts after Him and look at life from a spiritual perspective, they have unbelievable strength and satisfaction because they are doing God's work in God's way.

—N. B. W.

# growing your church God's way

Just around a treacherous curve on a rural road in Kentucky, a banner on the front of a church announces "We Are Growing God's Way." As I drove by that church and read the sign, my thoughts lingered on that idea for miles. I have no way of knowing if that church is making good on its promise, but the focus is right—God wants His Church in every setting to grow His way. And since God started the Church, owns the Church and maintains the Church, He knows how to nourish the congregations we serve.

Added to my Kentucky experience is a pastors' meeting in Oregon with some of the most selfless servants of Christ I have ever met. About 30 pastors came to pray, to think, to rekindle a fresh vision for their hard-to-grow churches (none had more than 100 people in attendance). After discussing many difficulties, one pastor with the glow of God on his face said, "Let's remember, living in one of the most secularized areas in the world means we have more spiritually needy prospects than most other places." God will honor such a perspective.

At some point in ministry every pastor must decide either to pursue growth or to start preaching that God doesn't care about numbers. I have been tempted by the latter thinking, but agree with a pastor friend of mine who often reminds his congregation, "We count people because people count." I like that. His concept is hard to resist in light of biblical teachings.

More recently, Rick Warren, founding pastor of the great Saddleback Church in Orange County, California, helps us all understand how a healthy church is a growing church. In his epic book *The Purpose Driven Church*, Warren suggests that a healthy church grows naturally just as a healthy child grows. The apostle Paul certainly agrees: "From [Christ] the whole body, joined and held together by every supporting ligament, grows and builds itself up in love, as each part does its work" (Eph. 4:16). God wants His Church to grow and He created health in her very nature.

I sometimes still think of that little Kentucky church, and I pray that it is in good health and growing naturally. I pray that the pastors I met in Oregon are happily experiencing God in His help to grow their churches. When growth is slow or stymied, the church's health must be examined and her illnesses healed.

These broodings took me back to the Bible where Jesus frequently taught how His kingdom grows. I was inspired again when I reread Jesus' examples from nature that show us the kind of growth He wants in His Church. Consider these precepts he gave for advancing Kingdom opportunities He entrusts to us:

*Everything starts with good seed.*
Even fertile ground that has been thoroughly prepared will not produce an abundant crop without good seed. Our Lord's parable of the soil in Matthew 13 teaches that all ground is not equally productive. Many ministers know firsthand about hard, stony, thorny ground. But in spite of soil conditions, nothing happens without good seed.

*The Lord's clear message is to keep sowing good seed.*
Sometimes Satan snatches the word of God from folks— that's hard soil. Sometimes new converts do not grow

roots—that's rocky soil. Sometimes wealth and other priorities choke out the gospel—that's thorny soil. But our Master Gardener encourages us. Seeds often multiply thirty-, sixty- or even a hundredfold. To grow an abundant harvest, sow gospel seed. Our seed is the Word of God.

I love Jesus' assurance to faithful pastors: "Some fell on good earth and came up with a flourish, producing a harvest exceeding his wildest dreams" (Mark 4:8, *THE MESSAGE*). Keep sowing.

*Water roots and cultivate plants.*
Few plants survive without cultivation and water. Though I do not understand how plants use sunlight and water to flourish and to produce a harvest, I know that's what happens. Water the gospel seed. Cultivate the tender plants. Do everything you know to help make your gospel garden grow. And God promises to give an increase.

Tender Kingdom plants are strengthened miraculously by worship that celebrates salvation, teaching that meets pressing needs and Christ-centered pastoral care that brings hope into life's crises.

*Expect a harvest.*
A small boy ruined his granddad's garden by digging up the seeds a few days after he planted them. He was eager to see if the seeds were growing. That's a sure way to harm Kingdom plants as well as Granddad's garden. Sometimes as pastors we just have to watch and wait.

Sow gospel seeds, cultivate the earth, and water the plants—and a harvest will naturally follow. Like farmers with their crops, we don't fully comprehend how the Kingdom grows, but it does.

As Jesus taught, Kingdom growth is dependable, but imperceptible. Growth in the plant kingdom is amazingly powerful—I recently saw a picture of a tiny Northern California redwood sapling that had split a cement parking lot. After we do all we can to assist the Kingdom growth, it is time to rely on the biblical teaching: "A man scatters seed on the ground. Night and day, whether he sleeps or gets up, the seed sprouts and grows, though he does not know how. All by itself the soil produces grain—first the stalk, then the head, then the full kernel in the head" (Mark 4:26-28).

Then Jesus adds, "As soon as the grain is ripe, he puts the sickle to it, because the harvest has come" (Mark 4:29).

Paul understood how to grow a church God's way. He wrote to the Corinthian church, "I planted the seed, Apollos watered it, but God made it grow" (1 Cor. 3:6). When God makes the gospel grow, the harvest is certain and the ripening crops desperately need harvesting hands like ours.

Listen again to our Lord's heartening, insistent words: "Open your eyes and take a good look at what's right in front of you. . . . It's harvest time" (John 4:35, *THE MESSAGE*).

—N. B. W.

# the never-say-die

# Pastor

who

impacts

the third

millennium

SECTION 6

# magnificent opportunities in the new century

Training pastors has been the passion of my soul during most of my ministry. My heart sings with joy when I realize that nearly 1,500 potential pastors have been in my classes, and 500 or more now serve congregations. Without realizing it, they taught me a lot about the Church and about younger generations.

For 10 of these years, I have edited a church-growth magazine for pastors. That privileged task allows me to observe ministry at the front lines. As editor, I have visited new churches, old churches, mission churches, multicultural churches, inner-city churches and suburban churches. I have developed friendships with ministers of all ages and educational levels. These selfless servants of Christ have strengthened my faith and challenged my commitment as I have seen them do heroic work for the gospel.

Recently, several former students, now my colleagues in ministry, asked me what I yearned to see happen in the Church at the start of this new century. After considerable thought, I made my list. Why not create your own list? Then use it as both a prayer list and a checklist for your future ministry.

*I long to see churches become an extended family.*
In an era when so many relationships are fractured, I believe the family of God can become an extended fami-

ly for persons who have no family or whose extended family live hundreds of miles away. It may be that our Christian families and churches show needy people what grace does in relationships. Cherish the human trophies of grace around you and welcome them in your heart as family. Acceptance and belonging are magnetic attributes for a church.

*I long to help the crying children.*
Our society does bad things to children. I want to take seriously Jesus' command to bring children to Him. I propose a plan to assign three mentors to each child in the church and neighborhood: (1) a Sunday School teacher, (2) an adult friend like a big brother or big sister, and (3) a prayer partner who prays daily for the child by name and keeps in touch by phone or mail. Even shut-ins can help with the third phase of this effort.

*I long to communicate the gospel to secularists.*
Masses of people seek acceptance, a way to start over, release from guilt, hope for tomorrow and a message of grace. I pray that the Church can show them how Jesus offers all this and infinitely more. Lonely and disillusioned people are desperately hungry for what God has already provided. The Church must go find them and introduce them to Christ, who has the answers. Hunger for God is universal, and the satisfaction of that hunger transforms individuals and creates growing churches.

*I long to help kindle mission passion for North America.*
Missions have come home to America. The Church in North America can find Christian immigrants and com-

mit to helping win them to Christ. If North America is really a mission field, as I believe it is, let's get passionately involved in winning the world next door with the same do-or-die fervor we have for winning Africa, Asia and India.

*I long for ministry to shape me into a Christ-quality person.*
Ministry can seem a frazzling, unending list of duties. But it is a privileged life that immerses me in Scripture and prayer. A former student wrote, "In ministry I get paid to study, pray and love people. What a deal!" He is right—ministry provides a pastor with the raw material for incredible personal spiritual development. The ministry is costly, but it also enriches us because we live so close to the spiritual action. I want to think of this intensity in a positive way, realizing that I have the occasion to grow more quickly by being a pastor.

*I hope to challenge every believer to become a person of prayer.*
Starting with myself, I want to make prayer an engaging experience. In place of making others feel guilty, I want to be made into a man of prayer so that people around me have only to watch me to see how important prayer is. I pray with humility that as God answers my prayers, the people He has given me will take great hope in going to the almighty God themselves.

*I long to invest one day a week in outreach.*
This vision calls for every pastor to set aside one day per week exclusively for outreach. That could change our world, recharge ministry, win thousands to Christ and keep established churches from lethal legalism.

*I long to experience a renewed sense of the supernatural.* I pray that God will send a renewed dependence on Him throughout the whole Body of Christ. I dream about renewal that seeks a holy anointing for preaching, a holy presence for pastoral care, a holy humility in the exercise of ecclesiastical power and a holy direction for administrative and leadership strategies.

This is a great time for impacting the world for Christ. Let's do it well.

—N. B. W.

# does "dear abby" preaching help anyone?

Preaching—what a task, what a privilege, what an audacity and what a miracle.

I recently heard Ted Koppel—the savvy TV commentator—tell a national conference of secular journalists that the Internet, satellite dishes, interactive TV and other coming advances in communication technology would force content and production to get much better. He warned that TV would have to make massive improvements, or it would have no audience.

Koppel started me thinking about communication and preaching. I wrestled with the question, "Can the old story be told more effectively?" Some people might fear that changing our communication methods will water down gospel truths. But being forced to communicate the message of the Great Commission more competently actually provides a great growth opportunity for us preachers. As I thought about Koppel's comment, I remembered George Buttrick's observation: "People are driven from the church not so much by stern truth that makes them uneasy, as by weak nothings that make them contemptuous."[1]

But what message does God want us to communicate? According to the Great Commission, preachers have a twofold assignment: to evangelize unbelievers and to teach believers that walking with Christ leads to a quality life, full of possibilities—

the kind of life intended when He created us. Simply stated, our Master directs the church to introduce unbelievers to the good news and to disciple believers. Everything we do is shaped by these two challenges. The content of Christian preaching is the gospel—pure, simple, transforming and wonderful. By proclaiming it in its fullness, we will both win and nurture people.

I have worked hard across many years to perfect my preaching. As I look back over more years than I care to count, I thank God for many positive influences that have shaped my preaching. My pastor taught me by example during my teen years. College, seminary and graduate studies in preaching and worship had a profound impact on me. Watching and listening to outstanding preachers have also greatly affected my preaching.

I have driven miles to hear great preachers, including Gerald Kennedy, E. Stanley Jones, Vance Havner, Warren Wiersbe, James E. Massey, Paul Rees, Haddon Robinson, Gardner Taylor, Max Lucado, Charles Stanley, Robert Schuller, Elton Trueblood, Lloyd Ogilvie, Rick Warren and Leith Anderson. And I have listened to hundreds of sermons on audiocassettes.

Books about preaching line my shelves. I have read several thousand printed sermons and helped to train more than 1,500 student preachers. Even now, I sometimes hear 60 student sermons in a 10-week period. Several years ago, I started the monthly sermon resource called *Preaching Today*, now produced by *Christianity Today*. So my quest to be an effective preacher has gone on for a long time.

With all these resources and all these experiences, I should be a superb preacher by now. And I want to be. But I need to improve. I want God to help me recognize my flaws and help me correct them.

Lately I've been thinking a lot about those who hear us preach. Just as patients have a bill of rights and airline passengers have theirs, I wonder if the average Christian shouldn't also have a bill of rights for preaching. Perhaps a preaching bill of rights for lay listeners would include the following:

*The right to biblically based preaching.*
Any preaching without strong scriptural roots is little more than a friendly pep talk. Advice on job security, family skills, how to get rich from tithing or how not to spend too much for Christmas is not biblical preaching. Preaching to human needs only produces eternal results when the needs and answers are authentically scriptural. We must not settle for outward trimmings, stripped of inward meaning. Enthusiasm for innovation in preaching is useful so long as the eternal Word of God is preached simply and understandably. Preaching the Bible puts us in touch with the central source of God's directives for us and His life-changing communication about Christ.

*The right to "encountered" preaching.*
Forgive the awkwardness of my expression, but it precisely suits my meaning. A preacher must experience an encounter with the passage during the preparation process. No one should preach from a passage until his or her life has been shaped by that portion of God's Word. By "encounter" I mean that preachers draw near holy ground and are so impacted by the burning bush that they carry the fire of God to His people.

*The right to authoritative preaching.*
Follow Billy Graham's example and speak God's truth loudly and clearly: "The Bible says . . ." Preach the truth

with anointing. And watch your hearers receive God's Word with gratitude.

*The right to preaching that is more than popular self-helps.*
When your church hears you preach, they should receive more than they can find in the self-help section at Barnes and Noble. Pop-psychology preaching is neither good preaching nor good psychology. Resist the temptation to preach self-help notions not connected to godliness or eternal life.

*The right to prepared preaching.*
Compelling preaching takes hours of preparation. Hang out with your Bibles, your books and your commitment to preach the eternal truth as found in Jesus. Your call to preach is a gift God wants you to use to enrich your relationship to Him and with His people. Here's how the process works: Prepared preaching takes you into the Word, the lives of people and the mission of the Church.

*The right to challenging preaching.*
The goal of entertainment is to allow an audience to relax, absorb and enjoy an event or happening without putting out much effort. Do not fall prey to the idea that the goal of your sermon is to entertain. Millions of Christians for 2,000 years have gladly responded to our Lord's invitation to come, to follow and, yes, to die. Tough demands of consecration, commitment and sacrifice attract people to Christ. Such a message is seldom entertaining.

*The right to preaching that addresses contemporary life.*
I met a church planter in the Netherlands whose church

grew from 10 to nearly 1,000 in 10 years. When I asked him his secret, he immediately replied: "I preach on themes secularists are hungry to hear—like starting again, forgiveness, a sense of belonging and a quality life. Everyone is eager to hear about these issues and how they impact their lives. That's why they come, and that's why they come back." My friend builds his church on the unique and attractive qualities of the gospel.

By unique qualities, I mean those characteristics that cannot be found elsewhere. Since those realities belong only to the Church, we must communicate them clearly and proclaim them joyously.

Preaching—what a task, what a privilege, what an audacity and what a miracle. I wholeheartedly agree with John Wycliffe who wrote in 1378, "Preaching the Word of God is as great as hearing it."[2]

—N. B. W.

**Notes**

1. Rebecca Davis and Susan Mesner, eds., *The Treasury of Religious and Spiritual Quotations* (Pleasantville, NY: Reader's Digest Association, 1994), p. 423.
2. Ibid., p. 426.

# call a truce to the worship wars

The worship war is real, though putting those words together—
"worship" and "war"—seems unthinkable. I once found these
words written by John Greenleaf Whittier in the front of a hymnal
in St. Martin-in-the-Fields in London: "To worship rightly is to
love each other, each hymn a smile and each kindly deed a prayer."

But the present state of some churches doesn't faintly
resemble these poetic words. In pastors' conferences and lay
leadership retreats, I sometimes ask, "Will you please raise your
hand if your church is having a worship war." The percentage of
hands in the air is astoundingly high—maybe 80 percent. These
wars dishonor Christ and confuse many good people.

While being interviewed on a radio talk show about my book
*Hunger for the Holy*, a telephone caller pushed me to discuss worship music. I resisted because her agenda had little to do with
the content of my book. Finally the caller said, "I'm glad you
agree with me about the awful music being brought into the
Church. At our church, as a protest, people from our Sunday
School class sit out the music part of the service. Then we go
into the sanctuary about the time the sermon starts." Though I
had tried to remain neutral, I expressed shock and regret that
such a spirit was displayed in any church.

If you can bear another story about the worship war, consider
this one. I received a letter from a long-term, now-retired church

musician who wrote, "At our church we have 'seven-eleven' music; we sing 7 words 11 times." Something to consider, isn't it?

As I grieve about the worship wars, I sometimes have a mental picture of all believers standing before the Judge of the Earth on the last day. As we gather, I envision Him saying, "Everyone who believed in singing out of the book, stand on this side. And everyone who sang off the wall, stand on that side." Then after all find their place, I think He might say, "Wasn't it stupid to be divided over this matter when the same amount of energy could have been used to better build My kingdom on earth?" When the emotion gets extracted from this issue, the disagreements sound like pure nonsense.

Still our churches war over worship. The battle sometimes rages in loud fury and sometimes simmers in quiet, seething resentment. But many Christians have stubbornly hardened their positions. Though we are all in the army of the Lord, our new recruits and old veterans are being wounded by friendly fire. Meanwhile, our enemy laughs and our Lord weeps.

We need a truce, a cease-fire, an armistice. Rather than wounding any more of our troops, we could agree to turn our firepower on the enemy by considering the following issues:

*Today versus 10 years from now.*
Those now adamant about a certain kind of music will face their own children in the churches of tomorrow. When this rising generation demands its new music, how will today's generation react? Will they deny their grandchildren the music they want? If our Lord tarries, it will happen.

*Message versus method.*
Obviously, modern technology must be used to make

sure our message is heard and understood. Most Christians agree that new methods must be used to communicate the changeless gospel. Keeping outdated strategies will cause us to miss the masses, but to change the message is spiritual suicide.

*Encounter versus entertainment.*
Church services that merely entertain are not worship. Music that produces a clapping, swinging response is not necessarily pleasing to God just because people like it and participate readily. Authentic corporate worship must produce a holy meeting with God—a unique, awe-inspiring, divine meeting that cannot be found anywhere outside the community of faith.

*Need-centered preaching versus needed preaching.*
For years, I have strongly advocated that effective preaching must speak to real needs real people feel. I believe that still. But there is a danger to so focus preaching on human problem solving that we neglect preaching on more needed themes. Preaching on themes like sin, salvation, holiness, faith, hope, love and peace is more needed than sermons on how to raise good kids, how to have a good marriage and how to make your boss happy. However, there is a wonderful meeting place between these two issues. If you are to raise truly good kids, you are out to teach them godliness and encourage them to rely on Christ. If you are going to have a good marriage, it will conform to scriptural principles. If you are going to make your true Boss happy, you will care less for human opinion than for the Lord's opinion.

*Our wants versus God's will.*

Worship wars usually spring from differences in personal preferences. What do boomers, busters, Gen X-ers, the elderly and the church leaders prefer in worship styles? That's the wrong question. The real question is, What does God want?

Jesus tells us that God is seeking worshipers who worship Him in spirit and in truth. When God examines our inner life, I'm sure He looks past the music style to see whether we come to Him humbly, desiring to know Him better and to obey Him more fully. In the glory of the throne room, all that is shallow and peripheral must go. Every worship form must pass the test of being worthy of His approval.

*Pastors versus worship leaders.*

Have you noticed that when we say the word "worship" these days, people immediately think of singing? Musicians function as worship leaders in most Christian services. But I wonder if this idea has been thoroughly thought through. I wonder how anyone can authentically lead worship who has not cared for straying sheep, interceded for the lost, married the young, buried the dead or carried the people's burdens to God in prayer?

*New people versus old saints.*

Do we possess a shred of evidence that these two groups need something different in worship? Surely, developing seeker-sensitive services does not mean crafting believer-alienating services. Surely, services designed to help believers mature do not repulse seekers. Can anyone conceive of Jesus saying, "If you don't like what we do in worship, learn to live with it or get out"? Any practice that really hinders a serious disciple of our Lord, regardless of age, needs to be evaluated, tweaked or changed. The same applies to new believers. New converts need veteran Christians and old hands need new believers. Dividing them doesn't seem like a good way to keep a church healthy.

*Reality versus emptiness.*
Every worship form can be empty or full, depending on the leader and the worshipers. If we want our worship forms to express our adoration of God, we must seek His guidance in our planning for music and our preparation for the pastoral prayer, and we must ask for His anointing on our preaching. Every true Christian believer desires and needs to experience reality in worship. Argument about worship forms usually start when meaning is missing.

Let's declare a cease-fire to the worship war. I beg you, pastor, to lay down your prejudices about worship. Let us find ways to lead people into the majestic, awesome, life-changing presence of our holy God. His welcome awaits us there.

—N. B. W.

# standing before ahab

When Elijah stood before Ahab (see 1 Kings 18), he had no idea what the consequences might be, but he knew he was doing what was right. He was obedient. He was vigilant. He was faithful. He was and still is a great example for all of us.

God's love stretches far beyond His people to those who live under the nose of our churches. He wants His gospel shared throughout the world. Towns and cities benefit wherever the Christian gospel goes. For too long, civic responsibility and spiritual passion have been separate in our actions and ministries. Of course, the primary task of the church is to preach the gospel, which changes hearts, and eventually behavior, because those hearts have been changed. However, pastors must ask another question: Am I doing the right thing in my community? We pastors must feel a holy compulsion to take a Christ-exalting stand regarding community issues. Do what you know to be right regardless of the consequences that may come to you. If pastors don't, who will?

As I have traveled along my journey of ministry, I have, many times, reflected on a few of the words of Bill and Gloria Gaither's song "There's Something about That Name"—"Jesus, Jesus, Jesus, Let all heaven and earth proclaim: Kings and kingdoms will all pass away, But there's something about that name!"[1] I have found a spine of steel in those words. At first the connection of the song and civic responsibility may not seem obvious. But those words are true. Only the kingdom of Jesus is eternal;

all else will pass away. So, when I speak up for Him, I speak up for a cause that will last forever. We are sometimes tricked into thinking that the real world is the world of everyday politics, educational battles and tax reform. However, as Christians, we surely know that the real world is Jesus' world, representing all that will never fade away, according to the Scriptures.

And so a pastor sometimes must move into the enemy's territory. Three examples come to mind from my ministry.

When I was pastoring in Salem, Oregon, a cult named Eckankar decided to move into our town. They focused their evangelistic efforts on young people, and I feared their influence on the youth of our city. On my daily radio program, I talked about the evils of this group and wrote a letter to the newspaper editor asking him, "Is there some way we can keep this godless cult out of our community?" My opposition aroused animosity, and my life was threatened. Considering the danger to my family, I wondered if standing up against this cult was worth the risks and intimidation.

But Eckankar never came to Salem, at least not as long as I lived in that city. Though they had the legal constitutional right to come, they chose not to do so because of negative public opinion. Salem was a better place because of our opposition. As a pastor, I helped give needed impetus to opposition of this group for the good of our town. And I am glad I did. But I must admit it was often a lonely road.

I remember another incident of intervention in civic affairs. When my dad was a pastor in St. Louis, legalized gambling wanted a foothold in our area and was going to install race tracks and pari-mutuel betting. My pastor dad took on the gambling industry in Missouri and East St. Louis, Illinois. I doubt that my father stopped to consider the possible consequences when he started. But before it was over, Mom and I were taken into protective custody until the controversy died down. I remember staying in a hotel in another state for several days. Gambling was kept out of the state, at least for a while. Now riverboat gambling is flourishing. No matter what the personal consequences, Dad felt he had to do what was right.

The third example is from my pastorate in Pasadena. I agreed to have a pro-life rally in our sanctuary. Christian leaders from many denominations, including the Roman Catholic churches, filled the place. It was bigger and the passions more intense than I had expected. Those who opposed the rally stood yelling on our sidewalks, defecating on driveways, carrying placards and blowing horns. The opposition was more than a protest; it was an out-of-control mob. Law-enforcement helicopters flew overhead and police personnel surrounded the church. I remember walking into my office and saying to myself, "What have you done now?" Though I served this church as pastor, I had no idea what the outcome of my decision would be for our members or for the community. Many in our congregation were unhappy with the press coverage we were getting, and they let me know it. Everywhere around me emotions were at breaking point. I seemed to be the lightning rod.

But when the rally began, speaker after speaker offered love and acceptance to the protesters. Rather than demean the opposition outside the building, the speakers prayed for them, loved them and said the best they could about them. We took a stand for authentic, loving righteousness that day. I saw hate melt in the name of Jesus. Our community was better because we had the rally, because we prayed and because we were not intimidated by the consequences. We did what we did because it needed to be done.

When I pulled the covers over me that night, I knew I had done the right thing. I slept well knowing I had been faithful, and that God would see us through this difficulty.

Let me ask, are you actively involved in some life-changing causes in your community? I pray that you are. Please understand, I am not proposing anything stupid or freakish, but I appeal for a new commitment to righteousness in our personal lives and in the lives of our communities. Many of our towns and cities are scandalized at the rampant secularization that is sweeping over them. You might be surprised at how many people in town would be willing to follow you if you, a pastor, are willing to lead the way. If you do not lead the way to righteousness, the next generation might be lost for all time.

Individuals must be won to Christ in the community, no doubt about it. But some social justice and moral issues must be tackled on a community level. They need dedication, organization and sometimes cooperation with other Christian churches. Perhaps every pulpit should announce clearly, "We've had enough. Everything else has been tried; it's time we turn to God." Here are several ways to start:

*Network with other believers.*
Discover what the Spirit is doing in your community, and cooperate with Him. Forces of righteousness must join to make improvements happen.

*Become informed.*
What needs to be done in your community? Let the gospel of Christ set your agenda so no social service agencies define Christian service for you. Form a social action committee to keep you renewed.

*Choose battles.*
As I have implied elsewhere, you do not have enough energy or insight for every battle. But everyone can do

something. Organize your efforts, so they make the greatest impact.

*Consider how much God loves your neighbors.*
Remember how patient He was with you. Recall how He came back again and again to draw you to himself. Kindness, loving attitudes and quiet speech all help attract reasonable people to the cause of Christ. If we believe righteousness produces the highest quality life, our way of living and our lifestyle witness must show that reality to neighbors and friends.

*Never despise smallness.*
I love the implications of Margaret Mead's brief sentence: "Never doubt that a small group of thoughtful, committed citizens can change the world."[2] If she is right, we must do what needs to be done to change our world.

*Ask God to look you over.*
Sometimes we shy away from asking what He thinks of us. But why? Why not find out what pleases Him and then do it?

—H. B. L.

## Notes

1. Gloria and William J. Gaither, "There's Something about That Name," *The Hymnal for Worship and Celebration* (Waco, TX: Word Music, 1986).
2. Jo Kadlecek, "How to Be a Better Neighbor," *Discipleship Journal*, no. 113 (September/October 1999), p. 60.

# honor your coworkers

I suffered surprising grief when our church, located in a steel mill town in California, hired its first staff person. I expected to be ecstatic, but I was sad. Before this young man came, the young people flocked around *me* after every service, and I thoroughly enjoyed their attention. Even though adding a youth pastor to our staff was my idea, I had second thoughts when he arrived. Just out of seminary, he was witty, gifted, handsome—and naturally moved into my place with the teens. I felt their affections shifting from me as they accepted him. My turf became his turf. And I had to step back to make it possible for the new leader to do his work.

From that experience and many others since then, I now realize that there are stages in ministry and that each phase should be maximized and enjoyed. When a church becomes too large for one person to care for all the needs, a senior pastor must relinquish a part of the ministry to someone else—whether another pastor, a staff member or a lay volunteer. There is a relief in the lightened load of duties, but there is a regret at the lessened satisfactions. A senior pastor who does not face this reality squarely can easily thwart staff efforts and become unhappy and frustrated.

Perhaps the most important part of staff development is to recruit exceptional people who are spiritually mature. One wise veteran pastor told me, "You have recruited the wrong staff member if you don't get someone who can do his or her specialty better than you can." Thus, securing a capable staff person is really an expression of your skills and wisdom. The purpose of a church staff is to expand and deepen ministry, not to flatter your ego or to serve as your "yes, sir" vassals in all you do.

Let me become scrupulously realistic. Developing a staff requires a commitment to helping others succeed. Even experienced staff need help to see how they fit a particular church. However, this mentoring, or coaching, effort is abundantly worthwhile because an effective staff provides rich improvements to the quality of a church's ministry and increases its spiritual vigor. However, if you choose the wrong person or refuse to relinquish ministry to that person's leadership or fail to invest the time necessary in helping new staff to adapt and become successful, you will create havoc. Your church will become confused about its mission, and you will be as unhappy as your staff and congregation.

I have worked with many wonderful staff members. Many are like family to me. They enriched my life and complemented my ministry beyond my ability to describe. On the other hand, I served with some who broke my heart. Or perhaps I should say they created heartache in their own lives and their failure had far-reaching effects on the faith of others in the church.

Don't forget that you are a pastor to your staff, as well as to the other believers in your congregation. Your willingness to invest in these men and women who help you in serving the church will have an exponential positive effect on the church. Mark it down; it is as sure as tomorrow's rising of the sun. If these hard-working, tireless servants are not fed and nourished, loved and encouraged, believed in and stimulated, they will not be able to do their ministry effectively.

Earlier I mentioned a youth pastor who was discovered to be a practicing homosexual and diagnosed with AIDS. It was my duty to tell him, "You can't work here anymore." But as his pastor, I had to help him find treatment and strongly urged him to seek God's forgiveness. I was the only pastor he had.

Several times I wept as I watched a staff couple's marriage dissolve because they did not give time and attention to their relationship. Then they sought and found affection in the arms of those who were not their marriage partners. Fallout from such disasters means that some children, teenagers and college kids will always be suspicious of the church. Experience with failures such as these compelled me to provide devoted pastoral care to staff and their families.

Some staffers will push you to the edge. From their perspective, rules, mission statements and team efforts do not apply to them. They run on their own track without considering where the church is going or what other staff members are doing. They want to go solo or have the whole team do everything their way. But, for staff and their ministries to function effectively there must be cohesiveness, cooperation and commitment to a common mission.

The most tragic staff problem is that of a staff member who falls out of love with Jesus. It happens to those who were not properly motivated to start with, regardless of their great ability, fine education and outstanding credentials. Sometimes it happens to ministry folks who have had a great past track record but who lose their love for God or His people. When that happens, ego gratification and selfishness shape their actions.

Powerless, I have agonized as staff members atrophy and shrivel in their souls. Age makes no difference—some are young, others middle-aged and still others near retirement. When their spirits start to sag, their efforts become ineffective; and those they serve realize something is wrong but can't figure out quite what it is. For some older staff members, years of ministry are sometimes totally invalidated because of such a loss of love for the Lord.

Deprivation of a close connection with God almost always creates crisis. How absurd it is for anyone to try to do the Lord's work without the Lord.

As a senior pastor, you can provide an effective remedy for all these potential problems if you take authentic spiritual leadership with your staff. If you meet regularly with them as a group and spend time with them individually, you will know what is taking place in their lives and their work. Push the young ones to grow and the more experienced to become more mature. Keep the importance of personal relationship to God constantly before them. Prod them to take time with God. Encourage them to invest creativity and energy into their marriages. Challenge them to be great parents. Help them discover ways to recharge their spirits and reenergize their commitments.

Try the following strategies to strengthen your staff team:

*Open your heart to them.*
Pray for your own attitude so that you can truly rejoice with every achievement a staff member makes. Neither crowd them nor hold them at arm's length. Don't keep administrative secrets from them. Let them in. Let them know how much you need them. Listen to their opinions, advice and anecdotes. Be a part of their lives and let them be a part of yours.

*Treat them as equals.*
Everyone knows the senior pastor has more authority and usually more experience than any other staff member. That's as it should be. But please, don't throw the weight of your position around. If you are an effective leader, your staff will follow you without being coerced

into doing so. And if you are a weak leader, you will only hinder your relationship if you remind them constantly that you are boss. Tell them often that you believe in their ability and training. Affirm them as specialists called to do a particular ministry in the church.

### Pray together.

Spiritual power and unity result when you pray for one another by name, out loud. If you have never experienced this, try praying with your staff and you will experience what I mean. Sometimes the most effective prayer times happen on Sunday mornings just before staffers move into their assignments. The beginning of staff meetings is also a good time to pray. And establish the practice of stopping to pray when a problem comes up.

### Have regular staff meetings.

Give high priority in your own schedule to staff meetings. I prefer weekly meetings. At staff meetings give everyone the opportunity to reflect on the work of the previous Sunday. Pray about things as you go, and assure one another of your mutual prayers during the week. Staff members can also provide a wonderful clearinghouse for laypersons who need pastoral care. A good portion of time in the meeting should be used to plan for the next Sunday.

### Insist on spiritual accountability.

I have found two ways to make accountability work well. I ask staff members to give a brief witness of their current relationship with the Father. This part of the meeting can open with a simple sentence: "What has God done for you personally in the last week?" The second way to strengthen accountability is to ask staff members to report at the staff meetings on the spiritual impact of programs and ministries under their supervision. For example, you might ask the youth minister, "How did the retreat last week enhance the mission of the church?" Or the pastor to senior adults might be asked, "How does the Bible study you started last week with seniors fit in with the long-term spiritual goals you have for the group?"

*Model loyalty.*
One of the most important issues of staff ministry is that staffers must be loyal to the senior pastor and to staff colleagues. Not even a hint of gossip can be expressed by staff members to lay leaders or members. However, if a senior pastor makes a big deal of this issue, a sense of suspicion develops among the team. A more effective way to build trust and confidentiality is for the senior pastor to model such loyalty to his staff in every possible situation. Then loyalty will beget loyalty naturally.

I would like to take an opportunity to thank all those former staff members and their families who blessed me through the years as we labored together for the cause of Christ. Each of you knows who you are. I am deeply indebted to you, and I love you with the love of Jesus.

—H. B. L.

# it's time to go public

The aftermaths of the Oklahoma City bombing and the Columbine shootings demonstrated that a trust in God is the only answer when disasters strike. Though we know faith works in the tight places, we need to go public with that good news. If we believe with all our hearts that God has answers to current crises, it is a malfeasance of duty not to speak up.

Our society is on moral skids and has to be stopped before we destroy ourselves. Radio smut peddler Howard Stern boasted that his prayers have been answered because "everything has come down to my level." Sad, if true. But can we reverse these trends? Can we raise society's standards, bring back the refining influence of godliness and turn pagan thinking back to dependence on God?

The picture is bleak. Grossly uninformed newscasters categorize born-again believers as brain-dead, cultural lowbrows or social misfits. Conservative Christians are described as rigid; while those who advocate abortion, euthanasia and homosexual marriage are considered moderates. The secular voices in our land have called out their message for so long and so loudly that even Christians now quake in silence before their misrepresentations.

How much longer will we allow the media to bombard us with heinous violence, erotic filth and morally repulsive talk shows? When will love, outrage, sanity and piety kick in so we shout from every pulpit, "Enough!"

Consider the amazing answers we have for addressing contemporary problems. Honesty, when government is corrupt.

Purity, when millions break their marriage vows. Sanctity of life, when gangs kill to get even. Reconciliation, when racism divides. Peace, when wars and rumors of wars capture the headlines. We have homes that will adopt unwanted babies; compassionate Christians who will give of their means to help the poor; honest businessmen who will pay their taxes and contribute to community needs. But we must speak up.

It's time to go public. There is a hunger for spirituality in our land. The time for timid response is past; the time for speaking the truth in love has arrived. And in the process, we need to hear Jesus say, "Be as cunning as a snake, inoffensive as a dove" (Matt. 10:16, *THE MESSAGE*).

It's time to reject any taboo that denies us our right to speak the gospel. In love, we must confront our society. Let's warm up our voices, gargle a little lemon juice and speak up. Through the power of the Spirit we must also call Christ's Church to action. When awakened, believers can make a mighty difference for good and right.

Let's take righteousness to the streets . . . speak up where it counts . . . live such beautiful lives that others hear us gladly . . . and saturate society with this message through conversations, newspapers, cable and commercial TV, school boards, letters and phone calls to civic leaders. Let's stop cursing the darkness and start lighting candles in every corner of society. Here's how:

*Proclaim personal conversion.*
The unconverted cannot transform a culture. Every attempt at human-inspired utopia has failed. If our society is to be transformed, thousands must experience a personal faith that influences their public life. Personal transformation by the grace of God in millions of indi-

viduals is what our society needs, and it will also satisfy the hunger of our souls.

### Resist labels and embrace realities.

Do we really believe the Christian life is superior? If yes is our answer, let's tear up the labels with which we categorize each other. Let's get past religious right, fundamentalism, liberalism, Calvinism and Wesleyanism. To replace our labels, let's bear the name of Christ and march under the Lord's banner of hope and righteousness. We preach Christ crucified, the hope of glory.

### State the facts about who we are.

Pastors and lay leaders may understand Christian jargon, but the man or woman on the street will not know what the word "covenant" means or where "Beulah land" is. One woman from Alcoholics Anonymous recently visited a Christian church service with a friend. The pastor was preaching on Ephesians 2, which speaks of aliens being brought near by the blood of Christ. When asked what she thought of the service, the woman replied, "It was okay, but I thought it was a little spooky, all that talk about aliens." Obviously, when she heard the word "aliens," she didn't think of those outside God's Church, but rather of illegal immigrants or little green men from Mars.

Our culture no longer has a Christian memory, and few common people know much about vital Christianity. Let's speak in language they understand. Let's go public to tell them who we are, what we believe and what we do. If they really understood the offer of the quality of life that Jesus Christ promises, they would be attracted to Him and to His promise for a new start.

### Give doctrine hands and feet.

Unless we keep on guard, Christianity will slide into a rational belief system with no grip on the soul and no challenge to the will. Doctrines, creeds and articles of faith are needed, but they must come alive in caring hearts, serving hands and generous souls. Doctrine and theology miss their purpose if they belong only to experts and professionals.

### Radiate joy through lifestyles.

In one of my pastorates, a new convert told me, "I think I want to be a Christian, but I am afraid I will become sad and blue and unhappy. I thought Christ changed all that." I rest my case.

### Go forward to the basics.

It's time to seek the wisdom of heaven and claim the courage of the Early Church. A renewal of the miraculous is needed in every church. Outsiders want to know what makes the Church uniquely different from all other organizations. We need to know what that unique gospel is, and we need to tell them. Let's remember that the supernatural need not be spectacular to be miraculous. Let's help everyone know about the resources for building a great life, which come from anointed preaching, guidance of the Holy Spirit and awe in worship.

It's time to go public. The world needs what we represent now. Going public will drastically improve our society, revolutionize our churches and give us amazing satisfaction.

—N. B. W.

# adding value when they come to church

Why do people go to church? What benefit do they receive? And why should they continue to attend? Here are three true stories. The names have been changed to protect the innocent.

Mary was a homebound caregiver for three years for her dying husband. He was a well-known churchman who pastored churches, wrote books, taught at a great university and even participated in the civil rights march to Selma, Alabama. While passing through this dark valley, she received periodic visits—about once each quarter—from her pastor. Two weeks following Tom's funeral, she attended a worship service at her church to begin her spiritual reentry process. In her first four Sundays back at church, she heard three challenges—pray more, give more to the building fund and attend evening service if you don't want it closed down. Mary had hoped for nourishment for her famished soul, but biblical themes such as hope, comfort, faith, empowerment, courage and victory were never mentioned.

Pastor Crane, retired after 40 years of effective ministry, wrote that his pastor is devoted, well trained and sharp. But Crane grieves because biblical ideas like full surrender, consecration, purity or maturing in Christ have not been mentioned in three years. Crane has serious concerns about the spiritual depth of the congregation where he worships.

Lee Ann introduced herself after I made an impassioned plea at a retreat for lay Christians to be faithful in supporting their pastor. She asked me privately what a mature believer should do when the meager diet offered in the regular services of a church made it difficult to grow spiritually. I questioned her in detail, fully expecting her to be a bad-attitude grumbler. Instead, I found her to be a serious disciple who hungered to know more about wholeness, prayer, holiness, faith, Christlikeness, healing and dying grace. Without intending to speak so bluntly, she blurted out, "I have gone home from every service for six weeks asking myself why I went." Then she answered her own question before I could reply, "I really don't know why."

Maybe all three of these faithful friends of the gospel were having a bad day. Maybe, since they are veteran believers, they should "get on board or get out." After all, as long as a pastor has a full house, why should the spiritual state of a single believer be a problem? The faulty reasoning says the many are more important than the few.

I believe every pastor must be responsible to feed all the people of God and give as much care to mature believers as to seekers or new converts. As pastors, we must conscientiously consider what God wants believers to experience when they come to church and make sure the church provides that nourishment. Every church must consciously commit to adding value to people's lives by becoming a magnetic spiritual resource center, where people receive what they cannot get anywhere else.

*Add value by creating awe-inspiring worship.*
Worship "in spirit and in truth," as Jesus put it, makes everyone aware of being in the presence of God. Such worship engenders a sense of wonder and awe that God welcomes us into His throne room. As Jesus said to the woman at the well, "[These] are the kind of worshipers the Father seeks" (John 4:23).

In authentic worship, each song, prayer or word points people to Christ. There is nothing cheap, mediocre, empty or dull. Every element of the service so completely honors our Lord that our worship is worthy of His approval. Such worship invites us as beggars to the King's smorgasbord of blessing.

*Add value by building acceptance.*
The need for acceptance and love is basic to every human being. God has taught His Church how to love. One of the marks of identity for the Church is the rich, full and complete family love she exhibits. Those outside the Church should stand in amazement as onlookers did in New Testament times when they observed how the Early Church members loved one another. Why not fan the flame of loving acceptance in your church, until welcome, belonging and acceptance are inspiring, firsthand experiences for everyone in your church?

*Add value by doing the basics brilliantly.*
American culture is good at deserting the old in favor of the new. New is magnificent, while the old is rusty and considered useless. However, thousands of church attendees may not understand or live out even the simple essentials of the Christian faith. Why not present the basics in such an appealing way that they will be new and relevant to contemporary people?

*Add value by living a beautiful life.*
Show people the magnetism of a Christ-centered life that infuses every dimension of living with beauty and purpose. Explain and model the attractive fact that liv-

ing the gospel makes all aspects of life immeasurably more satisfying—work, home, relationships and leisure.

*Add value by offering discipleship opportunities.*
What would happen if Sunday night services were revamped into growth and maturity meetings? Consider trying it for eight weeks. Why not develop seeker-sensitive services on Sunday morning and provide believer-empowerment services on Sunday night? Converts do not really discover the joys of living their faith until they have been discipled into a thoroughly Christian lifestyle.

Invest every effort to see that your church adds value to everyone's life. Identify the strong points of the Christian faith, which believers cannot find anywhere outside the Church; then develop strategies to provide those strengths to everyone who attends your church. Make them glad they came.

—N. B. W.

# the magic hope
# of christmas

That day I can remember hurting more than I ever have—before
or since. I was only 16 years old, but I felt much more excruciating pain than that caused by any old football injury or by a nagging headache—the kind of pain that never goes away. It even
gripped my throat and half choked me. To this day, whenever my
mind goes back to that incident that happened so long ago, I feel
pain.

Just before Easter that year, Dad was forced to leave the
church he pastored, and so I didn't go to church that Easter—I
had no church. Our family was crushed and confused. The problems rocked me to the core, since I was too young to get away but
old enough to know how much was going on. But it was my
mother who suffered the most, as long-term friends deserted us
as if we were infected with a deadly contagious disease. One day
the world was ours; the next it was covered with clouds.

The following fall I went off to college. Seven years later I had
finished seminary and, by God's grace, was serving in my first
pastorate. But there were some terribly painful times in between.

Walk back in time with me to see how hope healed my hurts.

The first Christmas after our family crisis, the faculty and
students of the Christian college I attended loved me. My raw
emotions had made me miserable, and I was not much fun to be
around. I didn't know with whom to talk or what to say. But that
year, Christian people opened their hearts to me and treated a
confused college freshman as somebody important, even though

I thought of myself as a nobody. People who lived near the college invited me to dinner. Fellow students asked me to go home for the holidays with them—in short, the extended family of God loved me and bandaged my wounds.

One Sunday evening at church I heard this wonderful message of hope: "Even though you may not think you are special, even though you may be going through pain and suffering, Christmas is the promise of hope. If you place yourself in God's hands, He will take care of you. He will repay those lost years. He is the God of hope—that is what Christmas means."

Fast forward in time nearly three decades to my pastoral years at Pasadena. One particular Christmas, for some unknown reason, I did not feel especially inspired by the holy season. I knew the crowds would be present for the Christmas festivities. Great music would attract them, and the music would take lots of time in the services. So I reasoned that I could make it without much preaching preparation. Though I am ashamed to admit it, I rationalized that since worshipers would be coming for the music, the preaching would not be particularly important for them.

Then the Holy Spirit, perhaps in sympathy for those who would have to sit through my poorly prepared sermons, seemed to say, "H. B., you know there will be more non-Christians in the Christmas services than you will have at any other Sunday in the year. You need to tell them that the birth of the Christ Child means there is hope that God gives us at Christmas. You know folks will be there who feel alone, afraid and sad. What will you have to say?" My mood soon changed, and I was inspired to preach the old miraculous Christmas story again. Though my message wasn't especially profound, it had great meaning for me because it was a reminder that I had the privilege of doing for others what God had done for me so many years before.

God's message came to me again that week: "Remember what I did for you when you were in college? Remember what I did for you that Christmas when you were so lonely, confused and angry? Why not give that same gift to somebody else this Christmas?" I did, and many who heard those Christmas sermons thanked me for the reminder of God's power to heal and to give hope.

Adjust your time machine again. Go back with me to my first church and my first Christmas in that church. The church was small and the music ordinary, both in content and in quality of performance. But we wanted to offer hope. So we put food baskets together. We made funny little gifts. We sang Christmas songs. We went out of our way to find people who needed us. We found practical ways to offer hope. And when it was over, the people said with tears in their eyes, "Pastor, we cannot remember when we've had such a special day with the Lord."

There you have three time capsules from my experience. All of them speak of hope at Christmas. Don't you wish the Christmas message could be spoken every day?

My dear pastor friend, remember those in your church and community who need Christmas hope. They won't be going on trips, receiving expensive presents or enjoying the warmth of hot chocolate around the fire at home in with their families. They are depressed, lonely and afraid. Some have lost loved ones. Some are sick and wonder if they will see another day. Some are praying for children who are a long way from God. Some have broken homes and crushed spirits. Some have sad hearts camouflaged by happy faces. They all need hope, and God has entrusted you with the message of the only hope of the world, Jesus Christ.

Because of their depth of pain and loneliness, many hurting individuals decide to try church on special days. Drug addicts, alcoholics, single parents, disenchanted secularists, isolated divorcees and forsaken senior citizens will be there. Some wonder if anyone cares, even God. Don't overlook them and go to the beautiful people. Don't neglect the lonely and hopeless. They need to know you care about them. They need to know God loves them.

Seasons like Christmas mean that a caring God sent His Son from heaven to rescue the lost and lonely. Dear pastor, you represent Christ to these people. Tell them what He would have you say, "I have come to offer you hope, love and a sense of belonging. I'm here to give hope to everyone, including the lonely, broken and dysfunctional."

My prayer is that you will not overlook those who need strength and faith. Show them how loved they are by God and by you. Think of ways you can identify those individuals and how you can remind them of the true meaning of the season.

*Make sure the story gets told.*
It's easy to allow the church to become so involved in special events that the Christmas message gets clouded. Make sure your preaching during Advent announces over and over that Christ is the hopeful center of Christmas. See to it that the message does not get lost in the tinsel and wrappings of the season.

*Control events.*
Refuse to allow big Christmas events to crowd out preaching about Christ. Preaching was here a long time before big events came into vogue and will be around until Christ returns. Though we are sometimes tempted to think of preaching as a foolish communication, it is God's most effective way of speaking the message of hope at Christmas. Make sure Christmas preaching has

high visibility and authentic preparation.

*Watch for hurting people.*
Be on the lookout for those who need you most and minister to them. One word of Christmas hope might transform a life. Though the excitement of the special activities may make Christmas a particularly happy time for you, remember those who need a kindly word and a reassuring promise that God is at work in their lives. Designate someone, or even a small group of persons, to help identify the most needy individuals and point them to hope.

*Use the phone on Christmas morning.*
Before your family festivities begin, call 10 or 15 people who will have nobody with them on Christmas or those who have suffered loss since last Christmas. Make your list ahead of time along with phone numbers. These calls can be made in less than an hour, and they will provide the incredible gift of yourself.

*Hope is a boomerang.*
Your Christmas will be enriched as you share the good news. Try it for one Christmas season, and you will make it part of every future Christmas. Pastors who dispense the hope of God transform the lives of others and enrich their own lives in the process.

Why Christmas? Because when people gather in your sanctuary to worship, every service speaks of the hope of Christmas!

—H. B. L.

# His hand was the only one available

All of us from time to time do foolish or even life-threatening things. That's what I did one Saturday evening in the mountains of Oregon. Occasionally my personality gets me in trouble because I have a tendency to live on the edge. That night I took a risk and almost lost my life.

I was due to preach on Sunday in my own pulpit. So, after speaking at the Saturday evening session of a laymen's retreat, I jumped into my car and headed home. It was raining, but I hardly thought about it. A short distance down the road, I noticed a small sign indicating a shortcut; and on impulse I took it. The road, which had seemed broad and smooth at first, was soon a wet, rainy logging road. It was about 8:30 P.M. and I was listening to an NBA basketball game between the Portland Trailblazers and the Phoenix Suns. On this unfamiliar road, I swerved on a sudden curve and suddenly found myself staring at a topsy-turvy world. I had turned my car over on its side—resting against the mountain.

Then I did exactly what safety experts say not to do. I left my vehicle and walked away into unfamiliar territory. A light snow began to fall. As I walked, the snow came in flurries; and before long, I was forging into an all-out blizzard. I was dressed in loafers, cotton pants and a leather jacket that I prized. I had a few dollars in my pocket, but that was useless where I was.

My situation was horrible and frightening. I was not equipped for winter. I did not know where I was going. Soon the muscles in my leg began to draw up in terrible pain. Though I did not realize it, I was walking farther and farther from civilization and away from anyone who might be looking for me.

When Beverley woke at about midnight, she was puzzled to find that I hadn't returned. She called my secretary, Sue McFadden, to check my schedule, to see if I was indeed supposed to return when she had expected me. The two women realized that I was gone much later than I should have been, so they called the lodge where I had been speaking. The staff told them that I had left around eight. By now, it was one o'clock in the morning, so they immediately sent out a search party to look for me.

Meanwhile, I had walked in a wide circle up and down the mountain in blizzardlike conditions from about 9:00 P.M. until 5:00 the next morning when, by God's providence, I found myself back at my automobile. The emergency flashers had drained the battery, so I could not start the motor for heat. I crawled into the car that was on its side against the mountain and tried to stabilize myself. I was lying in the car, shaking uncontrollably from the cold, when I saw headlights. The rescue party had found me. They put me in their car, turned my car upright, and took me home.

As I reflected upon the situation and pieced together information provided by others, I realized that the first house in my path, had I found it, was guarded by German shepherd dogs that might have eaten me alive. Had I gone further up the mountain, I would have frozen to death before someone found me. Neither possibility seemed attractive to me. I felt the undeniable protection of my Lord. As I walked those snow-covered roads, I remember promising God a lot of things. I would be a better father, a better husband, a better Christian. I had even called out, "Why me, God?" and heard only the echo of my own voice. There were times when I wanted to give up and stop walking, but something kept me moving. I know now who that Someone was.

When I got home, my physician was there to check me over. He said I had no frostbite and my extremities were fine. He suggested, "Get in the bathtub and get your temperature up," which I did. All this happened early Sunday morning, and our first service at church started at 9:30 A.M. Since there was no real reason to stay home, I went to church and preached. I had a story to tell.

The glory of the story is that when I finished the message in which I talked about the uncertainties of life and told my harrowing story, I suggested that all of us have moments in our lives we can't control or predict. I shared that unpredictable things can happen to anyone and that we must be sure our lives are pleasing to Christ so we have no fear in the tough times.

Many came forward to pray as I gave the invitation to renew their relationship with Christ. Among them was a good man who came to church to please his family but who had never made a personal profession of faith in Christ. But he liked me; he was my friend, and he identified with my predicament. As I stood in the pulpit and watched this man come forward, I was drawn to him. I prayed with him as he bowed in humility before Christ.

Later, as we talked, I asked him why he would choose a day like this to accept Christ into his life. His response was gratifyingly simple: "You know, I like you and I was touched by the fact that God saved you from a terrible fate." He continued, "I thought to myself that if the Lord really cared enough about you to rescue you, I decided to embrace Him. It was not just because He rescued you, but because I need someone to watch over me as well. I was moved by the fact there is a God who really cares, loves and desires the best for us."

I lived through a life-altering situation—one that I never want to repeat—but I thanked God that I could see someone I loved bow at the foot of the Cross and see for himself what a wonderful Lord God we serve, who often turns something painful into something wonderful.

Sometimes the only thing we have is divine providence, but that's more than enough. I urge you to maintain a simple but profound message in your ministry—God cares. Make it clear so everyone knows the Father loves and protects them. I have been thinking about ways to say that better, and here's what I have discovered:

*Preach how God's mercy protects us even when we make wrong turns.*

The longer I serve God, the more convinced I am that He cares for us many times when we are not even aware of our need of His help. I marvel at His care even when I have made bad choices and taken wrong roads.

*Tell your story.*

Past generations of preachers were careful not to mention their own struggles in the pulpit. The idea was to keep focused on God and not on ourselves. I understand and cherish that goal, as I hope you do. But I believe there are ways to tell our stories, while still keeping the focus on God's love and grace. It just depends on how you use that story. If you use it to bring glory to yourself, you are abusing your position in the pulpit. If, on the other hand, you use a story to show how gracious God has been to you, then a story about yourself can be a perfectly appropriate part of a good sermon. Our hearers sometimes need to know that we pastors are mere mortals who need God's protecting providence fully as much as they do.

### God protects us from ourselves.

God often guards us from ourselves. Even when we go against our best instincts, persisting in risky behavior, our Lord often protects us by His good grace from the consequences. The slush on that mountain road should have convinced me to turn back, but I didn't. And before that night was over, my life was absolutely out of control. Perhaps it took that desperate situation to remind me of the reality of His protecting providence. That divine protection is a message people need and want to hear.

### Finish well.

People are eager to know that the loving providence of the Lord will take us all the way home to heaven. He has promised to carry us victoriously to the end. I enjoy thinking about the apostle Paul's life and testimony near the end. His attitude was that it wasn't always easy, but he gave it his best.

### Out of control.

As we close this book, I remind myself, as well as all of you, my pastor colleagues, that there are many circumstances in the life of a minister in which we find ourselves completely out of control. At those places we realize that we have to lean on God, because He is all we have. But He is always more than enough.

God allows some out-of-our-control experiences into our lives to teach us that He has ultimate control.

He does it much better than we can. All we need to do is to grasp His hand. It is the same hand that reaches out to save us, to hold us, to protect us and to guide us. The old preacher was right: "I would rather be with God in the dark than by myself in the light."

—H. B. L.

for the *Sake*

of

new

beginnings

*EPILOGUE*

# for the sake
## of new beginnings

We find ourselves in a new millennium. It seems almost impossible that we no longer designate the details of our lives with a "19." Those days are gone forever. As we move forward, I cannot help but think back to the century that just ended.

I was born in the late 1930s to a gifted clergyman in Arkansas. I was an only child and watched my mom and dad find effectiveness in ministry, only to experience heartbreak in their relationship—which time and patience would one day heal. Through it all, I was witness to the grace of God in our family. I was thrilled when my dad's ministry was restored and he was given a second chance to impact his world for Christ to a greater degree than ever before.

In the late 1950s, I met Beverley at Pasadena College in California. In a few months, we were married as 19- and 20-year-old college sweethearts. We had no idea what the future would hold, but in time we felt His certain direction into full-time Christian service. Before we knew it, we were attending seminary in Kansas City, Missouri—an unlikely couple in very uncomfortable surroundings—but we made it, and within a few years we were in our very first church in Southern California.

Into our lives came our two sons—Bradley and Bryan. We could not have asked for two nicer guys. After they had completed college, they met and married their wives—Tammy and Susan—beautiful Christian women who gave birth to our four grandchildren—Taylor, Amanda, Hilary and Jeffrey. Our lives have been blessed beyond anything we could have expected.

Along our adventure of ministry through the 1900s and into this new century have been multitudes of friends, family, teachers, coaches, professors, colleagues and coworkers who have their handprints all over my life and professional journey. One of these serendipitous realities was the providential move of God that brought about the association with my cousin, James Dobson. Our mothers were sisters, our dads were pastors, and we were both only children who, through the efforts of our matriarchal parents, were together frequently through our formative years. And in 1954 we were rooming together in college and competing as siblings do.

After college, Jim married Shirley. They went their way, and we went ours. There was a period of nearly 20 years of our lives that we were on our own journeys—building careers, having families and establishing our own paths that would determine the course of our lives.

In 1985 something wonderful happened. Our two families were united again when I became their pastor in California. It was during our years together in Pasadena that the decision and dream to share in ministry at Focus on the Family was determined. It all began during a conversation about you—my pastor colleagues—and it was decided that Focus on the Family needed to be on the forefront in facilitating restoration and renewal in the lives of clergy families and to do all we could to help you better manage your time, your finances and your personal lives. And though there is never a promotion from the active pastorate, I have been favored with the best of two worlds: a pastoral career that has crossed three decades and now the privilege of being called a "pastor to pastors." What a life! I will ever be indebted to James Dobson for opening up a door to a new world for me. In these years I have attempted to be faithful to you and this new call in my life; and you have been affirming in return.

Another happy relationship has been with my colleague in ministry and partner in writing—Neil B. Wiseman. Our roads began to intersect back in the early 1960s when we were pastors under construction—he in the West and Southeast and I on the West Coast. We would bump into each other from time to time at conferences and conventions. In those early days, we didn't always agree on strategies and details of ministry. Our backgrounds and approaches to ministry were very different. But we always agreed, and still do, that love for ministry stands at the top of God's great gifts to a pastor.

It seemed to be God's providence that brought us back together in 1992. I was in the beginning stages of our Pastor to Pastor ministry at Focus on the Family and Neil was serving as a longtime, well-respected trainer of young pastors. We met one day and talked of our mutual concern for the clergy families across North America, and soon our first book, *Pastors at Risk*, emerged. It was published in 1993. Since that time there have been five other books. God has used our partnership to encourage and affirm thousands of pastors worldwide, and now several of the books have been published in other languages.

They say an author only has so many books in him. I know for a fact most of mine would still be unpublished if it were not for Neil Wiseman and his wonderful wife, Bonnie. They, like Beverley and I, live in Colorado Springs; and Neil is still hard at work building faith, character and pastoral skills into spiritual leaders for the next generation.

As I take a few moments of personal privilege to look back on my winding pathway, I know, like you, there have been some tough times, even moments of despair; but from where I stand now, I see mostly sunshine. And I see unmistakably the hand of God that has never failed me. Man, has He ever been faithful!

I remember my first Christmas in our little California church. I was a 20-something pastor sitting in a cubbyhole of an office. In the tiny sanctuary not far away, our ragtag choir was rehearsing for their Advent performance. As I sat and listened to them sing about the love of God, the Christ Child and the marvelous message from the choir of angels that spoke of hope, freedom and forgiveness, it seemed that our modestly talented choir had been transformed into a celestial body. It didn't matter that there were only 8 or 10 of them—they sounded like a heavenly host. It was the words they sang, the enthusiasm that radiated from them and the spirit of the Christ Child that surrounded them that made the difference. I was so proud to be called their pastor. I still am.

That moment seems like a hundred years ago, but in some ways it is as though it were yesterday. As I enter the first decade of the year 2000, I do so with the same expectancy and sense of adventure that I had long ago. I can hardly wait to see what God has in mind for His Church in the days and years ahead. I look not at the dark clouds that surround us nor at the evidence that could discourage us. I choose, rather, to walk out into the limitless expanse of time and space to see a God who is in control. He is the same yesterday, today and forever. I choose to see a Church filled with potential and promise. I see hundreds of young men and women who, in the mind of our Lord, have just what is needed to guide and love His Church into the tomorrows of the twenty-first century; men and women who will continue to take the title of pastor seriously and who, when they hear their name called, will swell with proper pride. I am honored that in four different congregations, over a span of some 30 years, there were many who called me pastor. What a privilege!

—H. B. L.

# Use These Books to Encourage Yourself and Others

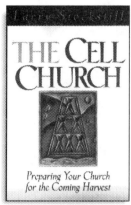
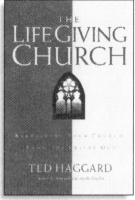
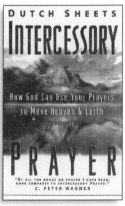

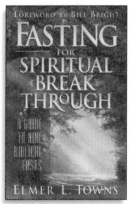

# Answers to Your Prayers

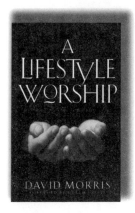

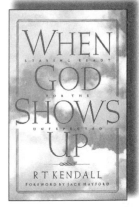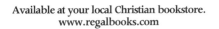